DARING

Only the insatiable curiosity of
Ray Bradbury would dare to probe
the lonely passions of:

a deep sea monster in his
attempts to make love to
a flirtatious foghorn

a misunderstood man of the
future with a perfectly
reasonable explanation for
murdering his house

a nubile young witch who
works out an ingenious method
for experiencing human love

"BRILLIANT, FASCINATING, ORIGINAL!"
CHICAGO TRIBUNE

Books by Ray Bradbury

Published by Bantam Books, Inc.

RAY BRADBURY

THE GOLDEN APPLES OF THE SUN

BANTAM BOOKS · TORONTO · NEW YORK · LONDON

*This low-priced Bantam Book
has been completely reset in a type face
designed for easy reading, and was printed
from new plates. It contains the complete
text of the original hard-cover edition.*

NOT ONE WORD HAS BEEN OMITTED.

THE GOLDEN APPLES OF THE SUN

*A Bantam Book / published by arrangement with
Doubleday & Company, Inc.*

PRINTING HISTORY

*Doubleday edition published March 1953
2nd printing .... April 1953*
Bantam edition published December 1954
*New Bantam edition published November 1961
2nd printing ... November 1961
3rd printing .... March 1967*
4th printing
5th printing

Several of the stories in this book appeared originally in THE NEW
YORKER, MADEMOISELLE, AMERICAN MERCURY, CHARM, THE REPORTER,
EPOCH, COLLIER'S *and* THE SATURDAY EVENING POST.

*The book title and the lines from "The Song of the Wandering
Aengus" from* The Wind Among the Reeds, *by W. B. Yeats, are
reprinted by permission of The Macmillan Company.*

*Bantam Books are published by Bantam Books, Inc., a subsidiary
of Grosset & Dunlap, Inc. Its trade-mark, consisting of the words
"Bantam Books" and the portrayal of a bantam, is registered in the
United States Patent Office and in other countries. Marca Registrada.
Bantam Books, Inc., 271 Madison Avenue, New York, N.Y. 10016.*

PRINTED IN THE UNITED STATES OF AMERICA

CONTENTS

And this one, with love, is for Neva,
daughter of Glinda
the Good Witch of the South

○

. . . And pluck till time and times are done
The silver apples of the moon,
The golden apples of the sun.
W. B. YEATS

1

THE FOG HORN

OUT THERE in the cold water, far from land, we waited every night for the coming of the fog, and it came, and we oiled the brass machinery and lit the fog light up in the stone tower. Feeling like two birds in the gray sky, McDunn and I sent the light touching out, red, then white, then red again, to eye the lonely ships. And if they did not see our light, then there was always our Voice, the great deep cry of our Fog Horn shuddering through the rags of mist to startle the gulls away like decks of scattered cards and make the waves turn high and foam.

"It's a lonely life, but you're used to it now, aren't you?" asked McDunn.

"Yes," I said. "You're a good talker, thank the Lord."

"Well, it's your turn on land tomorrow," he said, smiling, "to dance the ladies and drink gin."

"What do you think, McDunn, when I leave you out here alone?"

"On the mysteries of the sea." McDunn lit his pipe. It

was a quarter past seven of a cold November evening, the heat on, the light switching its tail in two hundred directions, the Fog Horn bumbling in the high throat of the tower. There wasn't a town for a hundred miles down the coast, just a road which came lonely through dead country to the sea, with few cars on it, a stretch of two miles of cold water out to our rock, and rare few ships.

"The mysteries of the sea," said McDunn thoughtfully. "You know, the ocean's the biggest damned snowflake ever? It rolls and swells a thousand shapes and colors, no two alike. Strange. One night, years ago, I was here alone, when all of the fish of the sea surfaced out there. Something made them swim in and lie in the bay, sort of trembling and staring up at the tower light going red, white, red, white across them so I could see their funny eyes. I turned cold. They were like a big peacock's tail, moving out there until midnight. Then, without so much as a sound, they slipped away, the million of them was gone. I kind of think maybe, in some sort of way, they came all those miles to worship. Strange. But think how the tower must look to them, standing seventy feet above the water, the God-light flashing out from it, and the tower declaring itself with a monster voice. They never came back, those fish, but don't you think for a while they thought they were in the Presence?"

I shivered. I looked out at the long gray lawn of the sea stretching away into nothing and nowhere.

"Oh, the sea's full." McDunn puffed his pipe nervously, blinking. He had been nervous all day and hadn't said why. "For all our engines and so-called submarines, it'll be ten thousand centuries before we set foot on the real bottom of the sunken lands, in the fairy kingdoms there, and know *real* terror. Think of it, it's still the year 300,000 Before Christ down under there. While we've paraded around with trumpets, lopping off each other's countries and heads, they have been living beneath the sea twelve miles deep and cold in a time as old as the beard of a comet."

"Yes, it's an old world."

"Come on. I got something special I been saving up to tell you."

We ascended the eighty steps, talking and taking our time. At the top, McDunn switched off the room lights so there'd be no reflection in the plate glass. The great eye of the light was humming, turning easily in its oiled socket. The Fog Horn was blowing steadily, once every fifteen seconds.

"Sounds like an animal, don't it?" McDunn nodded to himself. "A big lonely animal crying in the night. Sitting here on the edge of ten billion years calling out to the Deeps, I'm here, I'm here, I'm here. And the Deeps do answer, yes, they do. You been here now for three months, Johnny, so I better prepare you. About this time of year," he said, studying the murk and fog, "something comes to visit the lighthouse."

"The swarms of fish like you said?"

"No, this is something else. I've put off telling you because you might think I'm daft. But tonight's the latest I can put it off, for if my calendar's marked right from last year, tonight's the night it comes. I won't go into detail, you'll have to see it yourself. Just sit down there. If you want, tomorrow you can pack your duffel and take the motorboat in to land and get your car parked there at the dinghy pier on the cape and drive on back to some little inland town and keep your lights burning nights, I won't question or blame you. It's happened three years now, and this is the only time anyone's been here with me to verify it. You wait and watch."

Half an hour passed with only a few whispers between us. When we grew tired waiting, McDunn began describing some of his ideas to me. He had some theories about the Fog Horn itself.

"One day many years ago a man walked along and stood in the sound of the ocean on a cold sunless shore and said, 'We need a voice to call across the water, to warn ships; I'll make one. I'll make a voice like all of time and all of the fog that ever was; I'll make a voice that is like an empty bed beside you all night long, and like an empty house when you open the door, and like trees in autumn with no leaves. A sound like the birds flying south, crying, and a sound like November wind and the sea on the hard, cold shore. I'll make a sound that's so alone that no one can miss it, that whoever hears it will weep in their souls, and hearths will seem warmer, and being inside will seem better to all who hear it in the distant towns. I'll make me a sound and an apparatus and they'll call it a Fog Horn and whoever hears it will know the sadness of eternity and the briefness of life.' "

The Fog Horn blew.

"I made up that story," said McDunn quietly, "to try to explain why this thing keeps coming back to the lighthouse every year. The Fog Horn calls it, I think, and it comes. . . ."

"But——" I said.

"Sssst!" said McDunn. "There!" He nodded out to the Deeps.

Something was swimming toward the lighthouse tower.

It was a cold night, as I have said; the high tower was cold, the light coming and going, and the Fog Horn calling and calling through the raveling mist. You couldn't see far and you couldn't see plain, but there was the deep sea moving

3

on its way about the night earth, flat and quiet, the color of gray mud, and here were the two of us alone in the high tower, and there, far out at first, was a ripple, followed by a wave, a rising, a bubble, a bit of froth. And then, from the surface of the cold sea came a head, a large head, dark-colored, with immense eyes, and then a neck. And then—not a body—but more neck and more! The head rose a full forty feet above the water on a slender and beautiful dark neck. Only then did the body, like a little island of black coral and shells and crayfish, drip up from the subterranean. There was a flicker of tail. In all, from head to tip of tail, I estimated the monster at ninety or a hundred feet.

I don't know what I said. I said something.

"Steady, boy, steady," whispered McDunn.

"It's impossible!" I said.

"No, Johnny, *we're* impossible. *It's* like it always was ten million years ago. *It* hasn't changed. It's *us* and the land that've changed, become impossible. *Us!*"

It swam slowly and with a great dark majesty out in the icy waters, far away. The fog came and went about it, momentarily erasing its shape. One of the monster eyes caught and held and flashed back our immense light, red, white, red, white, like a disk held high and sending a message in primeval code. It was as silent as the fog through which it swam.

"It's a dinosaur of some sort!" I crouched down, holding to the stair rail.

"Yes, one of the tribe."

"But they died out!"

"No, only hid away in the Deeps. Deep, deep down in the deepest Deeps. Isn't *that* a word now, Johnny, a real word, it says so much: the Deeps. There's all the coldness and darkness and deepness in a word like that."

"What'll we do?"

"Do? We got our job, we can't leave. Besides, we're safer here than in any boat trying to get to land. That thing's as big as a destroyer and almost as swift."

"But here, why does it come *here?*"

The next moment I had my answer.

The Fog Horn blew.

And the monster answered.

A cry came across a million years of water and mist. A cry so anguished and alone that it shuddered in my head and my body. The monster cried out at the tower. The Fog Horn blew. The monster roared again. The Fog Horn blew. The monster opened its great toothed mouth and the sound that came from it was the sound of the Fog Horn itself. Lonely and vast and far away. The sound of isolation, a viewless sea, a cold night, apartness. That was the sound.

"Now," whispered McDunn, "do you know why it comes here?"

I nodded.

"All year long, Johnny, that poor monster there lying far out, a thousand miles at sea, and twenty miles deep maybe, biding its time, perhaps it's a million years old, this one creature. Think of it, waiting a million years; could *you* wait that long? Maybe it's the last of its kind. I sort of think that's true. Anyway, here come men on land and build this lighthouse, five years ago. And set up their Fog Horn and sound it and sound it out toward the place where you bury yourself in sleep and sea memories of a world where there were thousands like yourself, but now you're alone, all alone in a world not made for you, a world where you have to hide.

"But the sound of the Fog Horn comes and goes, comes and goes, and you stir from the muddy bottom of the Deeps, and your eyes open like the lenses of two-foot cameras and you move, slow, slow, for you have the ocean sea on your shoulders, heavy. But that Fog Horn comes through a thousand miles of water, faint and familiar, and the furnace in your belly stokes up, and you begin to rise, slow, slow. You feed yourself on great slakes of cod and minnow, on rivers of jellyfish, and you rise slow through the autumn months, through September when the fogs started, through October with more fog and the horn still calling you on, and then, late in November, after pressurizing yourself day by day, a few feet higher every hour, you are near the surface and still alive. You've got to go slow; if you surfaced all at once you'd explode. So it takes you all of three months to surface, and then a number of days to swim through the cold waters to the lighthouse. And there you are, out there, in the night, Johnny, the biggest damn monster in creation. And here's the lighthouse calling to you, with a long neck like your neck sticking way up out of the water, and a body like your body, and, most important of all, a voice like your voice. Do you understand now, Johnny, do you understand?"

The Fog Horn blew.

The monster answered.

I saw it all, I knew it all—the million years of waiting alone, for someone to come back who never came back. The million years of isolation at the bottom of the sea, the insanity of time there, while the skies cleared of reptile-birds, the swamps dried on the continental lands, the sloths and saber-tooths had their day and sank in tar pits, and men ran like white ants upon the hills.

The Fog Horn blew.

"Last year," said McDunn, "that creature swam round and round, round and round, all night. Not coming too near, puzzled, I'd say. Afraid, maybe. And a bit angry after coming all this way. But the next day, unexpectedly, the fog lifted, the sun came out fresh, the sky was as blue as a painting. And the monster swam off away from the heat and the silence and didn't come back. I suppose it's been brooding on it for a year now, thinking it over from every which way."

The monster was only a hundred yards off now, it and the Fog Horn crying at each other. As the lights hit them, the monster's eyes were fire and ice, fire and ice.

"That's life for you," said McDunn. "Someone always waiting for someone who never comes home. Always someone loving some thing more than that thing loves them. And after a while you want to destroy whatever that thing is, so it can't hurt you no more."

The monster was rushing at the lighthouse.

The Fog Horn blew.

"Let's see what happens," said McDunn.

He switched the Fog Horn off.

The ensuing minute of silence was so intense that we could hear our hearts pounding in the glassed area of the tower, could hear the slow greased turn of the light.

The monster stopped and froze. Its great lantern eyes blinked. Its mouth gaped. It gave a sort of rumble, like a volcano. It twitched its head this way and that, as if to seek the sounds now dwindled off into the fog. It peered at the lighthouse. It rumbled again. Then its eyes caught fire. It reared up, threshed the water, and rushed at the tower, its eyes filled with angry torment.

"McDunn!" I cried. "Switch on the horn!"

McDunn fumbled with the switch. But even as he flicked it on, the monster was rearing up. I had a glimpse of its gigantic paws, fishskin glittering in webs between the finger-like projections, clawing at the tower. The huge eye on the right side of its anguished head glittered before me like a caldron into which I might drop, screaming. The tower shook. The Fog Horn cried; the monster cried. It seized the tower and gnashed at the glass, which shattered in upon us.

McDunn seized my arm. "Downstairs!"

The tower rocked, trembled, and started to give. The Fog Horn and the monster roared. We stumbled and half fell down the stairs. "Quick!"

We reached the bottom as the tower buckled down toward us. We ducked under the stairs into the small stone cellar. There were a thousand concussions as the rocks rained down; the Fog Horn stopped abruptly. The monster crashed upon the tower. The tower fell. We knelt together, McDunn and I, holding tight, while our world exploded.

Then it was over, and there was nothing but darkness and the wash of the sea on the raw stones.

That and the other sound.

"Listen," said McDunn quietly. "Listen."

We waited a moment. And then I began to hear it. First a great vacuumed sucking of air, and then the lament, the bewilderment, the loneliness of the great monster, folded over and upon us, above us, so that the sickening reek of its body filled the air, a stone's thickness away from our cellar. The monster gasped and cried. The tower was gone. The light was gone. The thing that had called to it across a million years was gone. And the monster was opening its mouth and sending out great sounds. The sounds of a Fog Horn, again and again. And ships far at sea, not finding the light, not seeing anything, but passing and hearing late that night, must've thought: There it is, the lonely sound, the Lonesome Bay horn. All's well. We've rounded the cape.

And so it went for the rest of that night.

The sun was hot and yellow the next afternoon when the rescuers came out to dig us from our stoned-under cellar.

"It fell apart, is all," said Mr. McDunn gravely. "We had a few bad knocks from the waves and it just crumbled." He pinched my arm.

There was nothing to see. The ocean was calm, the sky blue. The only thing was a great algaic stink from the green matter that covered the fallen tower stones and the shore rocks. Flies buzzed about. The ocean washed empty on the shore.

The next year they built a new lighthouse, but by that time I had a job in the little town and a wife and a good small warm house that glowed yellow on autumn nights, the doors locked, the chimney puffing smoke. As for McDunn, he was master of the new lighthouse, built to his own specifications, out of steel-reinforced concrete. "Just in case," he said.

The new lighthouse was ready in November. I drove down alone one evening late and parked my car and looked across the gray waters and listened to the new horn sounding, once, twice, three, four times a minute far out there, by itself.

The monster?

It never came back.

7

"It's gone away," said McDunn. "It's gone back to the Deeps. It's learned you can't love anything too much in this world. It's gone into the deepest Deeps to wait another million years. Ah, the poor thing! Waiting out there, and waiting out there, while man comes and goes on this pitiful little planet. Waiting and waiting."

I sat in my car, listening. I couldn't see the lighthouse or the light standing out in Lonesome Bay. I could only hear the Horn, the Horn, the Horn. It sounded like the monster calling.

I sat there wishing there was something I could say.

2

THE PEDESTRIAN

To ENTER out into that silence that was the city at eight o'clock of a misty evening in November, to put your feet upon that buckling concrete walk, to step over grassy seams and make your way, hands in pockets, through the silences, that was what Mr. Leonard Mead most dearly loved to do. He would stand upon the corner of an intersection and peer down long moonlit avenues of sidewalk in four directions, deciding which way to go, but it really made no difference; he was alone in this world of 2053 A.D., or as good as alone, and with a final decision made, a path selected, he would stride off, sending patterns of frosty air before him like the smoke of a cigar.

Sometimes he would walk for hours and miles and return only at midnight to his house. And on his way he would see the cottages and homes with their dark windows, and it was not unequal to walking through a graveyard where only the faintest glimmers of firefly light appeared in flickers behind the windows. Sudden gray phantoms seemed to manifest upon inner room walls where a curtain was still undrawn against the night, or there were whisperings and murmurs where a window in a tomb-like building was still open.

Mr. Leonard Mead would pause, cock his head, listen, look, and march on, his feet making no noise on the lumpy walk. For long ago he had wisely changed to sneakers when strolling at night, because the dogs in intermittent squads would parallel his journey with barkings if he wore hard heels, and lights might click on and faces appear and an entire street be startled by the passing of a lone figure, himself, in the early November evening.

On this particular evening he began his journey in a westerly direction, toward the hidden sea. There was a good crystal frost in the air; it cut the nose and made the lungs blaze like a Christmas tree inside; you could feel the cold light going on and off, all the branches filled with invisible snow. He listened to the faint push of his soft shoes through autumn leaves with satisfaction, and whistled a cold quiet whistle between his teeth, occasionally picking up a leaf as he passed, examining its skeletal pattern in the infrequent lamplights as he went on, smelling its rusty smell.

"Hello, in there," he whispered to every house on every side as he moved. "What's up tonight on Channel 4, Channel 7, Channel 9? Where are the cowboys rushing, and do I see the United States Cavalry over the next hill to the rescue?"

The street was silent and long and empty, with only his shadow moving like the shadow of a hawk in mid-country. If he closed his eyes and stood very still, frozen, he could imagine himself upon the center of a plain, a wintry, windless Arizona desert with no house in a thousand miles, and only dry river beds, the streets, for company.

"What is it now?" he asked the houses, noticing his wrist watch. "Eight-thirty P.M.? Time for a dozen assorted murders? A quiz? A revue? A comedian falling off the stage?"

Was that a murmur of laughter from within a moon-white house? He hesitated, but went on when nothing more happened. He stumbled over a particularly uneven section of sidewalk. The cement was vanishing under flowers and grass. In ten years of walking by night or day, for thousands of miles, he had never met another person walking, not one in all that time.

He came to a cloverleaf intersection which stood silent where two main highways crossed the town. During the day it was a thunderous surge of cars, the gas stations open, a great insect rustling and a ceaseless jockeying for position as the scarab-beetles, a faint incense puttering from their exhausts, skimmed homeward to the far directions. But now these highways, too, were like streams in a dry season, all stone and bed and moon radiance.

He turned back on a side street, circling around toward his home. He was within a block of his destination when the lone car turned a corner quite suddenly and flashed a fierce white cone of light upon him. He stood entranced, not unlike a night moth, stunned by the illumination, and then drawn toward it.

A metallic voice called to him:

"Stand still. Stay where you are! Don't move!"

He halted.

"Put up your hands!"

"But——" he said.

"Your hands up! Or we'll shoot!"

The police, of course, but what a rare, incredible thing; in a city of three million, there was only *one* police car left, wasn't that correct? Ever since a year ago, 2052, the election year, the force had been cut down from three cars to one. Crime was ebbing; there was no need now for the police, save for this one lone car wandering and wandering the empty streets.

"Your name?" said the police car in a metallic whisper. He couldn't see the men in it for the bright light in his eyes.

"Leonard Mead," he said.

"Speak up!"

"Leonard Mead!"

"Business or profession?"

"I guess you'd call me a writer."

"No profession," said the police car, as if talking to itself. The light held him fixed, like a museum specimen, needle thrust through chest.

"You might say that," said Mr. Mead. He hadn't written in years. Magazines and books didn't sell any more. Everything went on in the tomb-like houses at night now, he thought, continuing his fancy. The tombs, ill-lit by television light, where the people sat like the dead, the gray or multi-colored lights touching their faces, but never really touching them.

"No profession," said the phonograph voice, hissing. "What are you doing out?"

"Walking," said Leonard Mead.

"Walking!"

"Just walking," he said simply, but his face felt cold.

"Walking, just walking, walking?"

"Yes, sir."

"Walking where? For what?"

"Walking for air. Walking to *see*."

"Your address!"

"Eleven South Saint James Street."

"And there is air *in* your house, you have an air *conditioner*, Mr. Mead?"

"Yes."

"And you have a viewing screen in your house to see with?"

"No."

"No?" There was a crackling quiet that in itself was an accusation.

"Are you married, Mr. Mead?"

"No."

"Not married," said the police voice behind the fiery beam. The moon was high and clear among the stars and the houses were gray and silent.

"Nobody wanted me," said Leonard Mead with a smile.

"Don't speak unless you're spoken to!"

Leonard Mead waited in the cold night.

"Just *walking,* Mr. Mead?"

"Yes."

"But you haven't explained for what purpose."

"I explained; for air, and to see, and just to walk."

"Have you done this often?"

"Every night for years."

The police car sat in the center of the street with its radio throat faintly humming.

"Well, Mr. Mead," it said.

"Is that all?" he asked politely.

"Yes," said the voice. "Here." There was a sigh, a pop. The back door of the police car sprang wide. "Get in."

"Wait a minute, I haven't done anything!"

"Get in."

"I protest!"

"Mr. Mead."

He walked like a man suddenly drunk. As he passed the front window of the car he looked in. As he had expected, there was no one in the front seat, no one in the car at all.

"Get in."

He put his hand to the door and peered into the back seat, which was a little cell, a little black jail with bars. It smelled of riveted steel. It smelled of harsh antiseptic; it smelled too clean and hard and metallic. There was nothing soft there.

"Now if you had a wife to give you an alibi," said the iron voice. "But——"

"Where are you taking me?"

The car hesitated, or rather gave a faint whirring click,

as if information, somewhere, was dropping card by punch-slotted card under electric eyes. "To the Psychiatric Center for Research on Regressive Tendencies."

He got in. The door shut with a soft thud. The police car rolled through the night avenues, flashing its dim lights ahead.

They passed one house on one street a moment later, one house in an entire city of houses that were dark, but this one particular house had all of its electric lights brightly lit, every window a loud yellow illumination, square and warm in the cool darkness.

"That's *my* house," said Leonard Mead.

No one answered him.

The car moved down the empty river-bed streets and off away, leaving the empty streets with the empty sidewalks, and no sound and no motion all the rest of the chill November night.

3

THE APRIL WITCH

Into the air, over the valleys, under the stars, above a river, a pond, a road, flew Cecy. Invisible as new spring winds, fresh as the breath of clover rising from twilight fields, she flew. She soared in doves as soft as white ermine, stopped in trees and lived in blossoms, showering away in petals when the breeze blew. She perched in a lime-green frog, cool as mint by a shining pool. She trotted in a brambly dog and barked to hear echoes from the sides of distant barns. She lived in new April grasses, in sweet clear liquids rising from the musky earth.

It's spring, thought Cecy. I'll be in every living thing in the world tonight.

Now she inhabited neat crickets on the tar-pool roads, now prickled in dew on an iron gate. Hers was an adaptably quick mind flowing unseen upon Illinois winds on this one evening of her life when she was just seventeen.

"I want to be in love," she said.

She had said it at supper. And her parents had widened

14

their eyes and stiffened back in their chairs. "Patience," had been their advice. "Remember, you're remarkable. Our whole family is odd and remarkable. We can't mix or marry with ordinary folk. We'd lose our magical powers if we did. You wouldn't want to lose your ability to 'travel' by magic, would you? Then be careful. Be careful!"

But in her high bedroom, Cecy had touched perfume to her throat and stretched out, trembling and apprehensive, on her four-poster, as a moon the color of milk rose over Illinois country, turning rivers to cream and roads to platinum.

"Yes," she sighed. "I'm one of an odd family. We sleep days and fly nights like black kites on the wind. If we want, we can sleep in moles through the winter, in the warm earth. I can live in anything at all—a pebble, a crocus, or a praying mantis. I can leave my plain, bony body behind and send my mind far out for adventure. Now!"

The wind whipped her away over fields and meadows.

She saw the warm spring lights of cottages and farms glowing with twilight colors.

If I can't be in love, myself, because I'm plain and odd, then I'll be in love through someone else, she thought.

Outside a farmhouse in the spring night a dark-haired girl, no more than nineteen, drew up water from a deep stone well. She was singing.

Cecy fell—a green leaf—into the well. She lay in the tender moss of the well, gazing up through dark coolness. Now she quickened in a fluttering, invisible amoeba. Now in a water droplet! At last, within a cold cup, she felt herself lifted to the girl's warm lips. There was a soft night sound of drinking.

Cecy looked out from the girl's eyes.

She entered into the dark head and gazed from the shining eyes at the hands pulling the rough rope. She listened through the shell ears to this girl's world. She smelled a particular universe through these delicate nostrils, felt this special heart beating, beating. Felt this strange tongue move with singing.

Does she know I'm here? thought Cecy.

The girl gasped. She stared into the night meadows.

"Who's there?"

No answer.

"Only the wind," whispered Cecy.

"Only the wind." The girl laughed at herself, but shivered.

It was a good body, this girl's body. It held bones of finest slender ivory hidden and roundly fleshed. This brain was like a pink tea rose, hung in darkness, and there was cider-wine in this mouth. The lips lay firm on the white, white teeth and the brows arched neatly at the world, and the hair blew soft and fine on her milky neck. The pores knit small and close. The nose tilted at the moon and the cheeks glowed like small fires. The body drifted with feather-balances from one motion to another and seemed always singing to itself. Being in this body, this head, was like basking in a hearth fire, living in the purr of a sleeping cat, stirring in warm creek waters that flowed by night to the sea.

I'll like it here, thought Cecy.

"What?" asked the girl, as if she'd heard a voice.

"What's your name?" asked Cecy carefully.

"Ann Leary." The girl twitched. "Now why should I say *that* out loud?"

"Ann, Ann," whispered Cecy. "Ann, you're going to be in love."

As if to answer this, a great roar sprang from the road, a clatter and a ring of wheels on gravel. A tall man drove up in a rig, holding the reins high with his monstrous arms, his smile glowing across the yard.

"Ann!"

"Is that you, Tom?"

"Who else?" Leaping from the rig, he tied the reins to the fence.

"I'm not speaking to you!" Ann whirled, the bucket in her hands slopping.

"No!" cried Cecy.

Ann froze. She looked at the hills and the first spring stars. She stared at the man named Tom. Cecy made her drop the bucket.

"Look what you've done!"

Tom ran up.

"Look what you *made* me do!"

He wiped her shoes with a kerchief, laughing.

"Get away!" She kicked at his hands, but he laughed again, and gazing down on him from miles away, Cecy saw the turn of his head, the size of his skull, the flare of his nose, the shine of his eye, the girth of his shoulder, and the hard strength of his hands doing this delicate thing with the handkerchief. Peering down from the secret attic of this lovely head, Cecy yanked a hidden copper ventriloquist's wire and the pretty mouth popped wide: "Thank you!"

"Oh, so you *have* manners?" The smell of leather on his hands, the smell of the horse rose from his clothes into the tender nostrils, and Cecy, far, far away over night meadows and flowered fields, stirred as with some dream in her bed.

"Not for you, no!" said Ann.

16

"Hush, speak gently," said Cecy. She moved Ann's fingers out toward Tom's head. Ann snatched them back.

"I've gone mad!"

"You have." He nodded, smiling but bewildered. "Were you going to touch me then?"

"I don't know. Oh, go away!" Her cheeks glowed with pink charcoals.

"Why don't you run? I'm not stopping you." Tom got up. "Have you changed your mind? Will you go to the dance with me tonight? It's special. Tell you why later."

"No," said Ann.

"Yes!" cried Cecy. "I've never danced. I want to dance. I've never worn a long gown, all rustly. I want that. I want to dance all night. I've never known what it's like to be in a woman, dancing; Father and Mother would never permit it. Dogs, cats, locusts, leaves, everything else in the world at one time or another I've known, but never a woman in the spring, never on a night like this. Oh, please—we *must* go to that dance!"

She spread her thought like the fingers of a hand within a new glove.

"Yes," said Ann Leary, "I'll go. I don't know why, but I'll go to the dance with you tonight, Tom."

"Now inside, quick!" cried Cecy. "You must wash, tell your folks, get your gown ready, out with the iron, into your room!"

"Mother," said Ann, "I've changed my mind!"

The rig was galloping off down the pike, the rooms of the farmhouse jumped to life, water was boiling for a bath, the coal stove was heating an iron to press the gown, the mother was rushing about with a fringe of hairpins in her mouth. "What's come over you, Ann? You don't like Tom!"

"That's true." Ann stopped amidst the great fever.

But it's spring! thought Cecy.

"It's spring," said Ann.

And it's a fine night for dancing, thought Cecy.

". . . for dancing," murmured Ann Leary.

Then she was in the tub and the soap creaming on her white seal shoulders, small nests of soap beneath her arms, and the flesh of her warm breasts moving in her hands and Cecy moving the mouth, making the smile, keeping the actions going. There must be no pause, no hesitation, or the entire pantomime might fall in ruins! Ann Leary must be kept moving, doing, acting, wash here, soap there, now out! Rub with a towel! Now perfume and powder!

17

"You!" Ann caught herself in the mirror, all whiteness and pinkness like lilies and carnations. *"Who are you to-night?"*

"I'm a girl seventeen." Cecy gazed from her violet eyes. "You can't see me. Do you know I'm here?"

Ann Leary shook her head. "I've rented my body to an April witch, for sure."

"Close, very close!" laughed Cecy. "Now, on with your dressing."

The luxury of feeling good clothes move over an ample body! And then the halloo outside.

"Ann, Tom's back!"

"Tell him to wait." Ann sat down suddenly. "Tell him I'm not going to that dance."

"What?" said her mother, in the door.

Cecy snapped back into attention. It had been a fatal relaxing, a fatal moment of leaving Ann's body for only an instant. She had heard the distant sound of horses' hoofs and the rig rambling through moonlit spring country. For a second she thought, I'll go find Tom and sit in his head and see what it's like to be in a man of twenty-two on a night like this. And so she had started quickly across a heather field, but now, like a bird to a cage, flew back and rustled and beat about in Ann Leary's head.

"Ann!"

"Tell him to go away!"

"Ann!" Cecy settled down and spread her thoughts.

But Ann had the bit in her mouth now. "No, no, I hate him!"

I shouldn't have left—even for a moment. Cecy poured her mind into the hands of the young girl, into the heart, into the head, softly, softly. *Stand up,* she thought.

Ann stood.

Put on your coat!

Ann put on her coat.

Now, march!

No! thought Ann Leary.

March!

"Ann," said her mother, "don't keep Tom waiting another minute. You get on out there now and no nonsense. What's come over you?"

"Nothing, Mother. Good night. We'll be home late."

Ann and Cecy ran together into the spring evening.

A room full of softly dancing pigeons ruffling their quiet, trailing feathers, a room full of peacocks, a room full of rainbow eyes and lights. And in the center of it, around, around, around, danced Ann Leary.

"Oh, it *is* a fine evening," said Cecy.

"Oh, it's a fine evening," said Ann.

"You're odd," said Tom.

The music whirled them in dimness, in rivers of song; they floated, they bobbed, they sank down, they arose for air, they gasped, they clutched each other like drowning people and whirled on again, in fan motions, in whispers and sighs, to "Beautiful Ohio."

Cecy hummed. Ann's lips parted and the music came out.

"Yes, I'm odd," said Cecy.

"You're not the same," said Tom.

"No, not tonight."

"You're not the Ann Leary I knew."

"No, not at all, at all," whispered Cecy, miles and miles away. "No, not at all," said the moved lips.

"I've the funniest feeling," said Tom.

"About what?"

"About you." He held her back and danced her and looked into her glowing face, watching for something. "Your eyes," he said, "I can't figure it."

"Do you see *me?*" asked Cecy.

"Part of you's here, Ann, and part of you's not." Tom turned her carefully, his face uneasy.

"Yes."

"Why did you come with me?"

"I didn't want to come," said Ann.

"Why, then?"

"Something made me."

"What?"

"I don't know." Ann's voice was faintly hysterical.

"Now, now, hush, hush," whispered Cecy. "Hush, that's it. Around, around."

They whispered and rustled and rose and fell away in the dark room, with the music moving and turning them.

"But you *did* come to the dance," said Tom.

"I did," said Cecy.

"Here." And he danced her lightly out an open door and walked her quietly away from the hall and the music and the people.

They climbed up and sat together in the rig.

"Ann," he said, taking her hands, trembling. "Ann." But the way he said the name it was as if it wasn't her name. He kept glancing into her pale face, and now her eyes were open again. "I used to love you, you know that," he said.

"I know."

"But you've always been fickle and I didn't want to be hurt."

"It's just as well, we're very young," said Ann.

"No, I mean to say, I'm sorry," said Cecy.

"What *do* you mean?" Tom dropped her hands and stiffened.

The night was warm and the smell of the earth shimmered up all about them where they sat, and the fresh trees breathed one leaf against another in a shaking and rustling.

"I don't know," said Ann.

"Oh, but *I* know," said Cecy. "You're tall and you're the finest-looking man in all the world. This is a good evening; this is an evening I'll always remember, being with you." She put out the alien cold hand to find his reluctant hand again and bring it back, and warm it and hold it very tight.

"But," said Tom, blinking, "tonight you're here, you're there. One minute one way, the next minute another. I wanted to take you to the dance tonight for old times' sake. I meant nothing by it when I first asked you. And then, when we were standing at the well, I knew something had changed, really changed, about you. You were different. There was something new and soft, something . . ." He groped for a word. "I don't know, I can't say. The way you looked. Something about your voice. And I know I'm in love with you again."

"No," said Cecy. "With me, with *me*."

"And I'm afraid of being in love with you," he said. "You'll hurt me again."

"I might," said Ann.

No, no, I'd love you with all my heart! thought Cecy. Ann, say it to him, say it for me. Say you'd love him with all your heart.

Ann said nothing.

Tom moved quietly closer and put his hand up to hold her chin. "I'm going away. I've got a job a hundred miles from here. Will you miss me?"

"Yes," said Ann and Cecy.

"May I kiss you good-by, then?"

"Yes," said Cecy before anyone else could speak.

He placed his iips to the strange mouth. He kissed the strange mouth and he was trembling.

Ann sat like a white statue.

"Ann!" said Cecy. "Move your arms, *hold* him!"

She sat like a carved wooden doll in the moonlight.

Again he kissed her lips.

"I do love you," whispered Cecy. "I'm here, it's me you saw in her eyes, it's me, and I love you if she never will."

He moved away and seemed like a man who had run a long distance. He sat beside her. "I don't know what's happening. For a moment there . . ."

"Yes?" asked Cecy.

"For a moment I thought——" He put his hands to his eyes. "Never mind. Shall I take you home now?"

"Please," said Ann Leary.

He clucked to the horse, snapped the reins tiredly, and drove the rig away. They rode in the rustle and slap and motion of the moonlit rig in the still early, only eleven o'clock spring night, with the shining meadows and sweet fields of clover gliding by.

And Cecy, looking at the fields and meadows, thought, It would be worth it, it would be worth everything to be with him from this night on. And she heard her parents' voices again, faintly, "Be careful. You wouldn't want to lose your magical powers, would you—married to a mere mortal? Be careful. You wouldn't want that."

Yes, yes, thought Cecy, even that I'd give up, here and now, if he would have me. I wouldn't need to roam the spring nights then, I wouldn't need to live in birds and dogs and cats and foxes, I'd need only to be with him. Only him. Only him.

The road passed under, whispering.

"Tom," said Ann at last.

"What?" He stared coldly at the road, the horse, the trees, the sky, the stars.

"If you're ever, in years to come, at any time, in Green Town, Illinois, a few miles from here, will you do me a favor?"

"Perhaps."

"Will you do me the favor of stopping and seeing a friend of mine?" Ann Leary said this haltingly, awkwardly.

"Why?"

"She's a good friend. I've told her of you. I'll give you her address. Just a moment." When the rig stopped at her farm she drew forth a pencil and paper from her small purse and wrote in the moonlight, pressing the paper to her knee. "There it is. Can you read it?"

He glanced at the paper and nodded bewilderedly.

"Cecy Elliott, 12 Willow Street, Green Town, Illinois," he said.

"Will you visit her someday?" asked Ann.

"Someday," he said.

"Promise?"

"What has this to do with us?" he cried savagely. "What do I want with names and papers?" He crumpled the paper into a tight ball and shoved it in his coat.

"Oh, please promise!" begged Cecy.

". . . promise . . ." said Ann.

"All right, all right, now let me be!" he shouted.

I'm tired, thought Cecy. I can't stay. I have to go home.

I'm weakening. I've only the power to stay a few hours out like this in the night, traveling, traveling. But before I go . . .

". . . before I go," said Ann.

She kissed Tom on the lips.

"This is *me* kissing you," said Cecy.

Tom held her off and looked at Ann Leary and looked deep, deep inside. He said nothing, but his face began to relax slowly, very slowly, and the lines vanished away, and his mouth softened from its hardness, and he looked deep again into the moonlit face held here before him.

Then he put her off the rig and without so much as a good night was driving swiftly down the road.

Cecy let go.

Ann Leary, crying out, released from prison, it seemed, raced up the moonlit path to her house and slammed the door.

Cecy lingered for only a little while. In the eyes of a cricket she saw the spring night world. In the eyes of a frog she sat for a lonely moment by a pool. In the eyes of a night bird she looked down from a tall, moon-haunted elm and saw the light go out in two farmhouses, one here, one a mile away. She thought of herself and her family, and her strange power, and the fact that no one in the family could ever marry any one of the people in this vast world out here beyond the hills.

"Tom?" Her weakening mind flew in a night bird under the trees and over deep fields of wild mustard. "Have you still got the paper, Tom? Will you come by someday, some year, sometime, to see me? Will you know me then? Will you look in my face and remember then where it was you saw me last and know that you love me as I love you, with all my heart for all time?"

She paused in the cool night air, a million miles from towns and people, above farms and continents and rivers and hills. "Tom?" Softly.

Tom was asleep. It was deep night; his clothes were hung on chairs or folded neatly over the end of the bed. And in one silent, carefully upflung hand upon the white pillow, by his head, was a small piece of paper with writing on it. Slowly, slowly, a fraction of an inch at a time, his fingers closed down upon and held it tightly. And he did not even stir or notice when a blackbird, faintly, wondrously, beat softly for a moment against the clear moon crystals of the windowpane, then, fluttering quietly, stopped and flew away toward the east, over the sleeping earth.

4

THE WILDERNESS

"OH, THE GOOD TIME has come at last——"

It was twilight, and Janice and Leonora packed steadily in their summer house, singing songs, eating little, and holding to each other when necessary. But they never glanced at the window where the night gathered deep and the stars came out bright and cold.

"Listen!" said Janice.

A sound like a steamboat down the river, but it was a rocket in the sky. And beyond that—banjos playing? No, only the summer-night crickets in this year 2003. Ten thousand sounds breathed through the town and the weather. Janice, head bent, listened. Long, long ago, 1849, this very street had breathed the voices of ventriloquists, preachers, fortunetellers, fools, scholars, gamblers, gathered at this self-same Independence, Missouri. Waiting for the moist earth to bake and the great tidal grasses to come up heavy enough to hold the weight of their carts, their wagons, their indiscriminate destinies, and their dreams.

> *"Oh, the Good Time has come at last,*
> *To Mars we are a-going, sir,*
> *Five Thousand Women in the sky,*
> *That's quite a springtime sowing, sir!"*

"That's an old Wyoming song," said Leonora. "Change the words and it's fine for 2003."

Janice lifted a matchbox of food pills, calculating the totals of things carried in those high-axled, tall-bedded wagons. For each man, each woman, incredible tonnages! Hams, bacon slabs, sugar, salt, flour, dried fruits, "pilot" bread, citric acid, water, ginger, pepper—a list as big as the land! Yet here, today, pills that fit a wrist watch fed you not from Fort Laramie to Hangtown, but all across a wilderness of stars.

Janice threw wide the closet door and almost screamed. Darkness and night and all the spaces between the stars looked out at her.

Long years ago two things had happened. Her sister had locked her, shrieking, in a closet. And, at a party, playing hide-and-seek, she had run through the kitchen and into a long dark hall. But it wasn't a hall. It was an unlit stair well, a swallowing blackness. She had run out upon empty air. She had pedaled her feet, screamed, and fallen! Fallen in midnight blackness. Into the cellar. It took a long while, a heartbeat, to fall. And she had smothered in that closet a long, long time without daylight, without friends, no one to hear her screamings. Away from everything, locked in darkness. Falling in darkness. Shrieking!

The two memories.

Now, with the closet door wide, with darkness like a velvet shroud hung before her to be stroked by a trembling hand, with the darkness like a black panther breathing there, looking at her with unlit eyes, the two memories rushed out. Space and a falling. Space and being locked away, screaming. She and Leonora working steadily, packing, being careful not to glance out the window at the frightening Milky Way and the vast emptiness. Only to have the long-familiar closet, with its private night, remind them at last of their destiny.

This was how it would be, out there, sliding toward the stars, in the night, in the great hideous black closet, screaming, but no one to hear. Falling forever among meteor clouds and godless comets. Down the elevator shaft. Down the nightmare coal chute into nothingness.

She screamed. None of it came out of her mouth. It collided upon itself in her chest and head. She screamed. She slammed the closet door! She lay against it! She felt the

24

darkness breathe and yammer at the door and she held it tight, eyes watering. She stood there a long time, until the trembling vanished, watching Leonora work. And the hysteria, thus ignored, drained away and away, and at last was gone. A wrist watch ticked, with a clean sound of normality, in the room.

"Sixty *million* miles." She moved at last to the window as if it were a deep well. "I can't believe that men on Mars, tonight, are building towns, waiting for us."

"The only thing to believe is catching our Rocket tomorrow."

Janice raised a white gown like a ghost in the room.

"Strange, strange. To marry—on another world."

"Let's get to bed."

"No! The call comes at midnight. I couldn't sleep, thinking how to tell Will I've decided to take the Mars Rocket. Oh, Leonora, think of it, my voice traveling sixty million miles on the lightphone to him. I changed my mind so quick—I'm scared!"

"Our *last* night on Earth."

Now they really knew and accepted it; now the knowledge had found them out. They were going away, and they might never come back. They were leaving the town of Independence in the state of Missouri on the continent of North America, surrounded by one ocean which was the Atlantic and another the Pacific, none of which could be put in their traveling cases. They had shrunk from this final knowledge. Now it was facing them. And they were struck numb.

"Our children, they won't be Americans, or Earth people at all. We'll all be Martians, the rest of our lives."

"I don't want to go!" cried Janice suddenly.

The panic froze her.

"I'm afraid! The space, the darkness, the Rocket, the meteors! *Everything* gone! Why should I go out there?"

Leonora took hold of her shoulders and held her close, rocking her. "It's a new world. It's like the old days. The men first and the women after."

"Why, why should I go, tell me!"

"Because," said Leonora at last, quietly, seating her on the bed, "Will is up there."

His name was good to hear. Janice quieted.

"These men make it so hard," said Leonora. "Used to be if a woman ran two hundred miles for a man it was something. Then they made it a thousand miles. And now they put a whole universe between us. But that can't stop us, can it?"

"I'm afraid I'll be a fool on the Rocket."

"I'll be a fool with you." Leonora got up. "Now, let's walk around town, let's see everything one last time."

Janice stared out at the town. "Tomorrow night this'll all be here, but we won't. People'll wake up, eat, work, sleep, wake again, but we won't know it, and they'll never miss us."

Leonora and Janice moved around each other as if they couldn't find the door.

"Come on."

They opened the door, switched off the lights, stepped out, and shut the door behind them.

In the sky there was a great coming-in and coming-in. Vast flowering motions, huge whistlings and whirlings, snowstorms falling. Helicopters, white flakes, dropping quietly. From west and east and north and south the women were arriving, arriving. Through all the night sky you saw helicopters blizzard down. The hotels were full, private homes were making accommodations, tent cities rose in meadows and pastures like strange, ugly flowers, and the town and the country were warm with more than summer tonight. Warm with women's pink faces and the sunburnt faces of new men watching the sky. Beyond the hills rockets tried their fire, and a sound like a giant organ, all its keys pressed upon at once, shuddered every crystal window and every hidden bone. You felt it in your jaw, your toes, your fingers, a shivering.

Leonora and Janice sat in the drugstore among unfamiliar women.

"You ladies look very pretty, but you sure look sad," said the soda-fountain man.

"Two chocolate malteds." Leonora smiled for both of them, as if Janice were mute.

They gazed at the chocolate drink as if it were a rare museum painting. Malts would be scarce for many years on Mars.

Janice fussed in her purse and took out an envelope reluctantly and laid it on the marble counter.

"This is from Will to me. It came in the Rocket mail two days ago. It was this that made up my mind for me, made me decide to go. I didn't tell you. I want you to see it now. Go ahead, read the note."

Leonora shook the note out of the envelope and read it aloud:

"Dear Janice: This is our house if you decide to come to Mars. Will."

Leonora tapped the envelope again, and a color photo-

26

graph dropped out, glistening, on the counter. It was a picture of a house, a dark, mossy, ancient, caramel-brown, comfortable house with red flowers and green cool ferns bordering it, and a disreputably hairy ivy on the porch.

"But, Janice!"

"What?"

"This is a picture of your house, here on Earth, here on Elm Street!"

"No. Look close."

And they looked again, together, and on both sides of the comfortable dark house and behind it was scenery that was not Earth scenery. The soil was a strange color of violet, and the grass was the faintest bit red, and the sky glowed like a gray diamond, and a strange crooked tree grew to one side, looking like an old woman with crystals in her white hair.

"That's the house Will's built for me," said Janice, "on Mars. It helps to look at it. All yesterday, when I had the chance, alone, and was most afraid and panicky, I took out this picture and looked at it."

They both gazed at the dark comfortable house sixty million miles away, familiar but unfamiliar, old but new, a yellow light shining in the right front parlor window.

"That man Will," said Leonora, nodding her head, "knows just what he's doing."

They finished their drinks. Outside, a vast warm crowd of strangers wandered by and the "snow" fell steadily in the summer sky.

They bought many silly things to take with them, bags of lemon candy, glossy women's magazines, fragile perfumes; and then they walked out into the town and rented two belted jackets that refused to recognize gravity and imitated only the moth, touched the delicate controls, and felt themselves whispered like white blossom petals over the town. "Anywhere," said Leonora, "anywhere at all."

They let the wind blow them where it would; they let the wind take them through the night of summer apple trees and the night of warm preparation, over the lovely town, over the houses of childhood and other days, over schools and avenues, over creeks and meadows and farms so familiar that each grain of wheat was a golden coin. They blew as leaves must blow below the threat of a fire-wind, with warning whispers and summer lightning crackling among the folded hills. They saw the milk-dust country roads where not so long ago they had drifted in moonlit helicopters in great whorls of sound spiraling down to touch beside cool night streams with the young men who were now gone.

They floated in an immense sigh above a town already made remote by the little space between themselves and the earth, a town receding behind them in a black river and coming up in a tidal wave of lights and color ahead, untouchable and a dream now, already smeared in their eyes with nostalgia, with a panic of memory that began before the thing itself was gone.

Blown quietly, eddying, they gazed secretly at a hundred faces of dear friends they were leaving behind, the lamplit people held and framed by windows which slid by on the wind, it seemed; all of Time breathing them along. There was no tree they did not examine for old confessions of love carved and whittled there, no sidewalk they did not skim across as over fields of mica-snow. For the first time they knew their town was beautiful and the lonely lights and the ancient bricks beautiful, and they both felt their eyes grow large with the beauty of this feast they were giving themselves. All floated upon an evening carrousel, with fitful drifts of music wafting up here and there, and voices calling and murmuring from houses that were whitely haunted by television.

The two women passed like needles, sewing one tree to the next with their perfume. Their eyes were too full, and yet they kept putting away each detail, each shadow, each solitary oak and elm, each passing car upon the small snaking streets below, until not only their eyes but their heads and then their hearts were too full.

I feel like I'm dead, thought Janice, and in the graveyard on a spring night and everything alive but me and everyone moving and ready to go on with life without me. It's like I felt each spring when I was sixteen, passing the graveyard and weeping for them because they were dead and it didn't seem fair, on nights as soft as that, that I was alive. I was guilty of living. And now, here, tonight, I feel they have taken me from the graveyard and let me go above the town just once more to see what it's like to be living, to be a town and a people, before they slam the black door on me again.

Softly, softly, like two white paper lanterns on a night wind, the women moved over their lifetime and their past, and over the meadows where the tent cities glowed and the highways where supply trucks would be clustered and running until dawn. They hovered above it all for a long time.

The courthouse clock was booming eleven forty-five when they came like spider webs floating from the stars, touching on the moonlit pavement before Janice's old house. The city was asleep, and Janice's house waited for them to come in searching for *their* sleep, which was not there.

28

"Is this *us*, here?" asked Janice. "Janice Smith and Leonora Holmes, in the year 2003?"

"Yes."

Janice licked her lips and stood straight. "I wish it was some other year."

"1492? 1612?" Leonora sighed, and the wind in the trees sighed with her, moving away. "It's always Columbus Day or Plymouth Rock Day, and I'll be darned if I know what we women can do about it."

"Be old maids."

"Or do just what we're doing."

They opened the door of the warm night house, the sounds of the town dying slowly in their ears. As they shut the door, the phone began to ring.

"The call!" cried Janice, running.

Leonora came into the bedroom after her and already Janice had the receiver up and was saying, "Hello, hello!" And the operator in a far city was readying the immense apparatus which would tie two worlds together, and the two women waited, one sitting and pale, the other standing, but just as pale, bent toward her.

There was a long pause, full of stars and time, a waiting pause not unlike the last three years for all of them. And now the moment had arrived, and it was Janice's turn to phone through millions upon millions of miles of meteors and comets, running away from the yellow sun which might boil or burn her words or scorch the meaning from them. But her voice went like a silver needle through everything, in stitches of talking, across the big night, reverberating from the moons of Mars. And then her voice found its way to a man in a room in a city there on another world, five minutes by radio away. And her message was this:

"Hello, Will. This is Janice!"

She swallowed.

"They say I haven't much time. A minute."

She closed her eyes.

"I want to talk slow, but they say talk fast and get it all in. So I want to say—I've decided. I will came up there. I'll go on the Rocket tomorrow. I *will* come up there to you, after all. And I love you. I hope you can hear me. I love you. It's been so long. . . ."

Her voice motioned on its way to that unseen world. Now, with the message sent, the words said, she wanted to call them back, to censor, to rearrange them, to make a prettier sentence, a fairer explanation of her soul. But already the words were hung between planets and if, by some cosmic radiation, they could have been illuminated, caught fire in vaporous wonder there, her love would have lit a dozen worlds and startled the night side of Earth into a premature dawn, she thought. Now the words were not hers at all, they belonged to space, they belonged to no one until they arrived, and they were traveling at one hundred and eighty-six thousand miles a second to their destination.

What will he say to me? What will he say back in *his* minute of time? she wondered. She fussed with and twisted the watch on her wrist, and the light-phone receiver on her ear crackled and space talked to her with electrical jigs and dances and audible auroras.

"Has he answered?" whispered Leonora.

"Shhh!" said Janice, bending, as if sick.

Then his voice came through space.

"I hear him!" cried Janice.

"What does he say?"

The voice called out from Mars and took itself through the places where there was no sunrise or sunset, but always the night with a sun in the middle of the blackness. And somewhere between Mars and Earth everything of the message was lost, perhaps in a sweep of electrical gravity rushing by on the flood tides of a meteor, or interfered with by a rain of silver meteors. In any event, the small words and the unimportant words of the message were washed away. And his voice came through saying only one word:

". . . love . . ."

After that there was the huge night again and the sound of stars turning and suns whispering to themselves and the sound of her heart, like another world in space, filling her earphones.

"Did you *hear* him?" asked Leonora.

Janice could only nod.

"What did he say, what did he say?" cried Leonora.

But Janice could not tell anyone; it was much too good to tell. She sat listening to that one word again and again, as her memory played it back. She sat listening, while Leonora took the phone away from her without her knowing it and put it down upon its hook.

Then they were in bed and the lights out and the night wind blowing through the rooms a smell of the long journey in darkness and stars, and their voices talking of tomorrow, and the days after tomorrow which would not be days at all, but day-nights of timeless time; their voices faded away into sleep or wakeful thinking, and Janice lay alone in her bed.

Is this how it was over a century ago, she wondered, when the women, the night before, lay ready for sleep, or not ready, in the small towns of the East, and heard the sound of horses in the night and the creak of the Conestoga wagons ready to go, and the brooding of oxen under the trees, and the cry of children already lonely before their time? All the sounds of arrivals and departures into the deep forests and fields, the blacksmiths working in their own red hells through midnight? And the smell of bacons and hams ready for the journeying, and the heavy feel of the wagons like ships foundering with goods, with water in the wooden kegs to tilt and slop across prairies, and the chickens hysterical in their slung-beneath-the-wagon crates, and the dogs running out to the wilderness ahead and, fearful, running back with a look of empty space in their eyes? Is this, then, how it was so long ago? On the rim of the precipice, on the edge of the cliff of stars. In their time the smell of buffalo, and in our time the smell of the Rocket. Is this, then, how it was?

And she decided, as sleep assumed the dreaming for her, that yes, yes indeed, very much so, irrevocably, this was as it had always been and would forever continue to be.

5

THE FRUIT AT THE BOTTOM OF THE BOWL

WILLIAM ACTON rose to his feet. The clock on the mantel
ticked midnight.

He looked at his fingers and he looked at the large room
around him and he looked at the man lying on the floor.
William Acton, whose fingers had stroked typewriter keys
and made love and fried ham and eggs for early breakfasts,
had now accomplished a murder with those same ten whorled
fingers.

He had never thought of himself as a sculptor and yet, in
this moment, looking down between his hands at the body
upon the polished hardwood floor, he realized that by some
sculptural clenching and remodeling and twisting of human
clay he had taken hold of this man named Donald Huxley
and changed his physiognomy, the very frame of his body.

With a twist of his fingers he had wiped away the exacting
glitter of Huxley's gray eyes; replaced it with a blind dullness
of eye cold in socket. The lips, always pink and sensuous,

were gaped to show the equine teeth, the yellow incisors, the nicotined canines, the gold-inlaid molars. The nose, pink also, was now mottled, pale, discolored, as were the ears. Huxley's hands, upon the floor, were open, pleading for the first time in their lives, instead of demanding.

Yes, it was an artistic conception. On the whole, the change had done Huxley a share of good. Death made him a handsomer man to deal with. You could talk to him now and he'd have to listen.

William Acton looked at his own fingers.

It was done. He could not change it back. Had anyone heard? He listened. Outside, the normal late sounds of street traffic continued. There was no banging of the house door, no shoulder wrecking the portal into kindling, no voices demanding entrance. The murder, the sculpturing of clay from warmth to coldness was done, and nobody knew.

Now what? The clock ticked midnight. His every impulse exploded him in a hysteria toward the door. Rush, get away, run, never come back, board a train, hail a taxi, get, go, run, walk, saunter, but get the blazes *out* of here!

His hands hovered before his eyes, floating, turning.

He twisted them in slow deliberation; they felt airy and feather-light. Why was he staring at them this way? he inquired of himself. Was there something in them of immense interest that he should pause now, after a successful throttling, and examine them whorl by whorl?

They were ordinary hands. Not thick, not thin, not long, not short, not hairy, not naked, not manicured and yet not dirty, not soft and yet not callused, not wrinkled and yet not smooth; not murdering hands at all—and yet not innocent. He seemed to find them miracles to look upon.

It was not the hands as hands he was interested in, nor the fingers as fingers. In the numb timelessness after an accomplished violence he found interest only in the *tips* of his fingers.

The clock ticked upon the mantel.

He knelt by Huxley's body, took a handkerchief from Huxley's pocket, and began methodically to swab Huxley's throat with it. He brushed and massaged the throat and wiped the face and the back of the neck with fierce energy. Then he stood up.

He looked at the throat. He looked at the polished floor. He bent slowly and gave the floor a few dabs with the handkerchief, then he scowled and swabbed the floor; first, near the head of the corpse; secondly, near the arms. Then he polished the floor all around the body. He polished the floor one yard from the body on all sides. Then he polished the floor two yards from the body on all sides. Then he polished the floor three yards from the body in all directions. Then he——

He stopped.

There was a moment when he saw the entire house, the mirrored halls, the carved doors, the splendid furniture; and, as clearly as if it were being repeated word for word, he heard Huxley talking and himself just the way they had talked only an hour ago.

Finger on Huxley's doorbell. Huxley's door opening.

"Oh!" Huxley shocked. "It's *you*, Acton."

"Where's my wife, Huxley?"

"Do you think I'd tell you, really? Don't stand out there, you idiot. If you want to talk business, come in. Through that door. There. Into the library."

Acton had *touched* the library door.

"Drink?"

"I need one. I can't believe Lily is gone, that she——"

"There's a bottle of burgundy, Acton. Mind fetching it from that cabinet?"

Yes, fetch it. *Handle* it. *Touch* it. He did.

"Some interesting first editions there, Acton. Feel this binding. *Feel* of it."

"I didn't come to see books, I——"

He had *touched* the books and the library table and *touched* the burgundy bottle and burgundy glasses.

Now, squatting on the floor beside Huxley's cold body with the polishing handkerchief in his fingers, motionless, he stared at the house, the walls, the furniture about him, his eyes widening, his mouth dropping, stunned by what he realized and what he saw. He shut his eyes, dropped his head, crushed the handkerchief between his hands, wadding it, biting his lips with his teeth, pulling in on himself.

The fingerprints were everywhere, *everywhere!*

"Mind getting the burgundy, Acton, eh? The burgundy bottle, eh? With your fingers, eh? I'm terribly tired. You understand?"

A pair of gloves.

Before he did one more thing, before he polished another area, he must have a pair of gloves, or he might unintentionally, after cleaning a surface, redistribute his identity.

He put his hands in his pockets. He walked through the house to the hall umbrella stand, the hatrack. Huxley's overcoat. He pulled out the overcoat pockets.

No gloves.

His hands in his pockets again, he walked upstairs, moving with a controlled swiftness, allowing himself nothing frantic, nothing wild. He had made the initial error of not wearing gloves (but, after all, he hadn't *planned* a murder, and his subconscious, which may have known of the crime before its commitment, had not even hinted he might need gloves before the night was finished), so now he had to sweat for his sin of omission. Somewhere in the house there must be at least one pair of gloves. He would have to hurry; there was every chance that someone might visit Huxley, even at this hour. Rich friends drinking themselves in and out the door, laughing, shouting, coming and going without so much as hello-good-by. He would have until six in the morning, at the outside, when Huxley's friends were to pick Huxley up for the trip to the airport and Mexico City. . . .

Acton hurried about upstairs opening drawers, using the handkerchief as blotter. He untidied seventy or eighty drawers in six rooms, left them with their tongues, so to speak, hanging out, ran on to new ones. He felt naked, unable to do anything until he found gloves. He might scour the entire house with the handkerchief, buffing every possible surface where fingerprints might lie, then accidentally bump a wall here or there, thus sealing his own fate with one microscopic, whorling symbol! It would be putting his stamp of approval on the murder, that's what it would be! Like those waxen seals in the old days when they rattled papyrus, flourished ink, dusted all with sand to dry the ink, and pressed their signet rings in hot crimson tallow at the bottom. So it would be if he left one, mind you, *one* fingerprint upon the scene! His approval of the murder did not extend as far as affixing said seal.

More drawers! Be quiet, be curious, be careful, he told himself.

At the bottom of the eighty-fifth drawer he found gloves.

"Oh, my Lord, my Lord!" He slumped against the bureau, sighing. He tried the gloves on, held them up, proudly flexed them, buttoned them. They were soft, gray, thick, impregnable. He could do all sorts of tricks with hands now and leave no trace. He thumbed his nose in the bedroom mirror, sucking his teeth.

"NO!" cried Huxley.

What a wicked plan it had been.

Huxley had fallen to the floor, *purposely!* Oh, what a wickedly clever man! Down onto the hardwood floor had dropped Huxley, with Acton after him. They had rolled and tussled and clawed at the floor, printing and printing it with their frantic fingertips! Huxley had slipped away a few feet, Acton crawling after to lay hands on his neck and squeeze until the life came out like paste from a tube!

Gloved, William Acton returned to the room and knelt

35

down upon the floor and laboriously began the task of swabbing every wildly infested inch of it. Inch by inch, inch by inch, he polished and polished until he could almost see his intent, sweating face in it. Then he came to a table and polished the leg of it, on up its solid body and along the knobs and over the top. He came to a bowl of wax fruit, burnished the filigree silver, plucked out the wax fruit and wiped them clean, leaving the fruit at the bottom unpolished.

"I'm *sure* I didn't touch *them*," he said.

After rubbing the table he came to a picture frame hung over it.

"I'm certain I didn't touch *that*," he said.

He stood looking at it.

He glanced at all the doors in the room. Which doors had he used tonight? He couldn't remember. Polish all of them, then. He started on the doorknobs, shined them all up, and then he curried the doors from head to foot, taking no chances. Then he went to all the furniture in the room and wiped the chair arms.

"That chair you're sitting in, Acton, is an old Louis XIV piece. *Feel* that material," said Huxley.

"I didn't come to talk furniture, Huxley! I came about Lily."

"Oh, come off it, you're not that serious about her. She doesn't love you, you know. She's told me she'll go with me to Mexico City tomorrow."

"You and your money and your damned furniture!"

"It's nice furniture. Acton; be a good guest and feel of it."

Fingerprints can be found on fabric.

"Huxley!" William Acton stared at the body. "Did you guess I was going to kill you? Did your subconscious suspect, just as my subconscious suspected? And did your subconscious tell you to make me run about the house handling, touching, *fondling* books, dishes, doors, chairs? Were you *that* clever and *that* mean?"

He washed the chairs dryly with the clenched handkerchief. Then he remembered the body—he hadn't dry-washed *it*. He went to it and turned it now this way, now that, and burnished every surface of it. He even shined the shoes, charging nothing.

While shining the shoes his face took on a little tremor of worry, and after a moment he got up and walked over to that table.

He took out and polished the wax fruit at the bottom of the bowl.

"Better," he whispered, and went back to the body.

But as he crouched over the body his eyelids twitched and

his jaw moved from side to side and he debated, then he got up and walked once more to the table.

He polished the picture frame.

While polishing the picture frame he discovered——

The wall.

"That," he said, "is *silly*."

"Oh!" cried Huxley, fending him off. He gave Acton a shove as they struggled. Acton fell, got up, *touching* the wall, and ran toward Huxley again. He strangled Huxley. Huxley died.

Acton turned steadfastly from the wall, with equilibrium and decision. The harsh words and the action faded in his mind; he hid them away. He glanced at the four walls.

"Ridiculous!" he said.

From the corners of his eyes he saw something on one wall.

"I refuse to pay attention," he said to distract himself. "The next room, now! I'll be methodical. Let's see—altogether we were in the hall, the library, *this* room, and the dining room and the kitchen."

There was a spot on the wall behind him.

Well, *wasn't* there?

He turned angrily. "All right, all right, just to be *sure*," and he went over and couldn't find any spot. Oh, a *little* one, yes, right—*there*. He dabbed it. It wasn't a fingerprint anyhow. He finished with it, and his gloved hand leaned against the wall and he looked at the wall and the way it went over to his right and over to his left and how it went down to his feet and up over his head and he said softly, "No." He looked up and down and over and across and he said quietly, "That would be too much." How many square feet? "I don't give a good damn," he said. But unknown to his eyes, his gloved fingers moved in a little rubbing rhythm on the wall.

He peered at his hand and the wallpaper. He looked over his shoulder at the other room. "I must go in there and polish the essentials," he told himself, but his hand remained, as if to hold the wall, or himself, up. His face hardened.

Without a word he began to scrub the wall, up and down, back and forth, up and down, as high as he could stretch and as low as he could bend.

"Ridiculous, oh my Lord, ridiculous!"

But you must be certain, his thought said to him.

"Yes, one *must* be certain," he replied.

He got one wall finished, and then . . .

He came to another wall.

"What time *is* it?"

He looked at the mantel clock. An hour gone. It was five after one.

The doorbell rang.

Acton froze, staring at the door, the clock, the door, the clock.

Someone rapped loudly.

A long moment passed. Acton did not breathe. Without new air in his body he began to fail away, to sway; his head roared a silence of cold waves thundering onto heavy rocks.

"Hey, in there!" cried a drunken voice. "I know you're in there, Huxley! Open up, dammit! This is Billy-boy, drunk as an owl, Huxley, old pal, drunker than *two* owls."

"Go away," whispered Acton soundlessly, crushed against the wall.

"Huxley, you're in there, I hear you *breathing!*" cried the drunken voice.

"Yes, I'm in here," whispered Acton, feeling long and sprawled and clumsy on the floor, clumsy and cold and silent. "Yes."

"Hell!" said the voice, fading away into mist. The footsteps shuffled off. "Hell . . ."

Acton stood a long time feeling the red heart beat inside his shut eyes, within his head. When at last he opened his eyes he looked at the new fresh wall straight ahead of him and finally got courage to speak. "Silly," he said. "This wall's flawless. I won't touch it. Got to hurry. Got to hurry. Time, time. Only a few hours before those damn-fool friends blunder in!" He turned away.

From the corners of his eyes he saw the little webs. When his back was turned the little spiders came out of the wood-work and delicately spun their fragile little half-invisible webs. Not upon the wall at his left, which was already washed fresh, but upon the three walls as yet untouched. Each time he stared directly at them the spiders dropped back into the woodwork, only to spindle out as he retreated. "Those walls are all right," he insisted in a half shout. "I won't *touch* them!"

He went to a writing desk at which Huxley had been seated earlier. He opened a drawer and took out what he was look-ing for. A little magnifying glass Huxley sometimes used for reading. He took the magnifier and approached the wall uneasily.

Fingerprints.

"But those aren't mine!" He laughed unsteadily. "I *didn't* put them there! I'm *sure* I didn't! A servant, a butler, or a maid perhaps!"

The wall was full of them.

"Look at this one here," he said. "Long and tapered, a woman's, I'd bet money on it."

"Would you?"

"I would!"

"Are you certain?"

"Yes!"

"Positive?"

"Well—yes."

"Absolutely?"

"Yes, damn it, yes!"

"Wipe it out, anyway, why don't you?"

"There, by God!"

"Out damned spot, eh, Acton?"

"And this one, over here," scoffed Acton. "That's the print of a fat man."

"Are you sure?"

"Don't start *that* again!" he snapped, and rubbed it out. He pulled off a glove and held his hand up, trembling, in the glary light.

"Look at it, you idiot! See how the whorls go? See?"

"That proves nothing!"

"Oh, all right!" Raging, he swept the wall up and down, back and forth, with gloved hands, sweating, grunting, swearing, bending, rising, and getting redder of face.

He took off his coat, put it on a chair.

"Two o'clock," he said, finishing the wall, glaring at the clock.

He walked over to the bowl and took out the wax fruit and polished the ones at the bottom and put them back, and polished the picture frame.

He gazed up at the chandelier.

His fingers twitched at his sides.

His mouth slipped open and the tongue moved along his lips and he looked at the chandelier and looked away and looked back at the chandelier and looked at Huxley's body and then at the crystal chandelier with its long pearls of rainbow glass.

He got a chair and brought it over under the chandelier and put one foot up on it and took it down and threw the chair, violently, laughing, into a corner. Then he ran out of the room, leaving one wall as yet unwashed.

In the dining room he came to a table.

"I want to show you my Gregorian cutlery, Acton," Huxley had said. Oh, that casual, that *hypnotic* voice!

"I haven't time," Acton said. "I've got to see Lily——"

"Nonsense, look at this silver, this exquisite craftsmanship."

Acton paused over the table where the boxes of cutlery were laid out, hearing once more Huxley's voice, remembering all the touchings and gesturings.

Now Acton wiped the forks and spoons and took down all

the plaques and special ceramic dishes from the wall itself. . . .

"Here's a lovely bit of ceramics by Gertrude and Otto Natzler, Acton. Are you familiar with their work?"

"It *is* lovely."

"Pick it up. Turn it over. See the fine thinness of the bowl, hand-thrown on a turntable, thin as eggshell, incredible. And the amazing volcanic glaze. Handle it, *go* ahead. *I* don't mind."

HANDLE IT. GO AHEAD. PICK IT UP!

Acton sobbed unevenly. He hurled the pottery against the wall. It shattered and spread, flaking wildly, upon the floor.

An instant later he was on his knees. Every piece, every shard of it, must be found. Fool, fool, fool! he cried to himself, shaking his head and shutting and opening his eyes and bending under the table. Find every piece, idiot, not one fragment of it must be left behind. Fool, fool! He gathered them. Are they all here? He looked at them on the table before him. He looked under the table again and under the chairs and the service bureaus and found one more piece by match light and started to polish each little fragment as if it were a precious stone. He laid them all out neatly upon the shining polished table.

"A lovely bit of ceramics, Acton. Go ahead—*handle* it."

He took out the linen and wiped it and wiped the chairs and tables and doorknobs and windowpanes and ledges and drapes and wiped the floor and found the kitchen, panting, breathing violently, and took off his vest and adjusted his gloves and wiped the glittering chromium. . . . "I want to show you my house, Acton," said Huxley. "Come along. . . ." And he wiped all the utensils and the silver faucets and the mixing bowls, for now he had forgotten what he had touched and what he had not. Huxley and he had lingered here, in the kitchen, Huxley prideful of its array, covering his nervousness at the presence of a potential killer, perhaps wanting to be near the knives if they were needed. They had idled, touched this, that, something else—there was no remembering what or how much or how many—and he finished the kitchen and came through the hall into the room where Huxley lay.

He cried out.

He had forgotten to wash the fourth wall of the room! And while he was gone the little spiders had popped from the fourth unwashed wall and swarmed over the already clean walls, dirtying them again! On the ceilings, from the chandelier, in the corners, on the floor, a million little whorled webs hung billowing at his scream! Tiny, tiny little webs, no bigger than, ironically, your—finger!

As he watched, the webs were woven over the picture frame, the fruit bowl, the body, the floor. Prints wielded the

40

paper knife, pulled out drawers, touched the table top, touched, touched, touched everything everywhere.

He polished the floor wildly, wildly. He rolled the body over and cried on it while he washed it, and got up and walked over and polished the fruit at the bottom of the bowl. Then he put a chair under the chandelier and got up and polished each little hanging fire of it, shaking it like a crystal tambourine until it tilted bellwise in the air. Then he leaped off the chair and gripped the doorknobs and got up on other chairs and swabbed the walls higher and higher and ran to the kitchen and got a broom and wiped the webs down from the ceiling and polished the bottom fruit of the bowl and washed the body and doorknobs and silverware and found the hall banister and followed the banister upstairs.

Three o'clock! Everywhere, with a fierce, mechanical intensity, clocks ticked! There were twelve rooms downstairs and eight above. He figured the yards and yards of space and time needed. One hundred chairs, six sofas, twenty-seven tables, six radios. And under and on top and behind. He yanked furniture out away from walls and, sobbing, wiped them clean of years-old dust, and staggered and followed the banister up, up the stairs, handling, erasing, rubbing, polishing, because if he left one little print it would reproduce and make a million more!—and the job would have to be done all over again and now it was four o'clock!—and his arms ached and his eyes were swollen and staring and he moved sluggishly about, on strange legs, his head down, his arms moving, swabbing and rubbing, bedroom by bedroom, closet by closet. . . .

They found him at six-thirty that morning.

In the attic.

The entire house was polished to a brilliance. Vases shone like glass stars. Chairs were burnished. Bronzes, brasses, and coppers were all aglint. Floors sparkled. Banisters gleamed.

Everything glittered. Everything shone, everything was bright!

They found him in the attic, polishing the old trunks and the old frames and the old chairs and the old carriages and toys and music boxes and vases and cutlery and rocking horses and dusty Civil War coins. He was half through the attic when the police officer walked up behind him with a gun.

"Done!"

On the way out of the house Acton polished the front doorknob with his handkerchief and slammed it in triumph!

6

INVISIBLE BOY

SHE TOOK the great iron spoon and the mummified frog and gave it a bash and made dust of it, and talked to the dust while she ground it in her stony fists quickly. Her beady gray bird-eyes flickered at the cabin. Each time she looked, a head in the small thin window ducked as if she'd fired off a shotgun.

"Charlie!" cried Old Lady. "You come outa there! I'm fixing a lizard magic to unlock that rusty door! You come out now and I won't make the earth shake or the trees go up in fire or the sun set at high noon!"

The only sound was the warm mountain light on the high turpentine trees, a tufted squirrel chittering around and around on a green-furred log, the ants moving in a fine brown line at Old Lady's bare, blue-veined feet.

"You been starving in there two days, darn you!" she panted, chiming the spoon against a flat rock, causing the plump gray miracle bag to swing at her waist. Sweating sour, she rose and marched at the cabin, bearing the pulverized flesh. "Come out, now!" She flicked a pinch of powder inside the lock. "All right, I'll come get you!" she wheezed.

She spun the knob with one walnut-colored hand, first one way, then the other. "O Lord," she intoned, "fling this door wide!"

When nothing flung, she added yet another philter and held her breath. Her long blue untidy skirt rustled as she peered into her bag of darkness to see if she had any scaly monsters there, any charm finer than the frog she'd killed months ago for such a crisis as this.

She heard Charlie breathing against the door. His folks had pranced off into some Ozark town early this week, leaving him, and he'd run almost six miles to Old Lady for company —she was by way of being an aunt or cousin or some such, and he didn't mind her fashions.

But then, two days ago, Old Lady, having gotten used to the boy around, decided to keep him for convenient company. She pricked her thin shoulder bone, drew out three blood pearls, spat wet over her right elbow, tromped on a crunch-cricket, and at the same instant clawed her left hand at Charlie, crying, "My son you are, you are my son, for all eternity!"

Charlie, bounding like a startled hare, had crashed off into the bush, heading for home.

But Old Lady, skittering quick as a gingham lizard, cornered him in a dead end, and Charlie holed up in this old hermit's cabin and wouldn't come out, no matter how she whammed door, window, or knothole with amber-colored fist or trounced her ritual fires, explaining to him that he was certainly her son *now*, all right.

"Charlie, you *there?*" she asked, cutting holes in the door planks with her bright little slippery eyes.

"I'm all of me here," he replied finally, very tired.

Maybe he would fall out on the ground any moment. She wrestled the knob hopefully. Perhaps a pinch too much frog powder had grated the lock wrong. She always overdid or underdid her miracles, she mused angrily, never doing them just *exact*, Devil take it!

"Charlie, I only wants someone to night-prattle to, someone to warm hands with at the fire. Someone to fetch kindling for me mornings, and fight off the spunks that come creeping of early fogs! I ain't got no fetchings on you for myself, son, just for your company." She smacked her lips. "Tell you what, Charles, you come out and I *teach* you things!"

"What things?" he suspicioned.

43

"Teach you how to buy cheap, sell high. Catch a snow weasel, cut off its head, carry it warm in your hind pocket. There!"

"Aw," said Charlie.

She made haste. "Teach you to make yourself shotproof. So if anyone bangs at you with a gun, nothing happens."

When Charlie stayed silent, she gave him the secret in a high fluttering whisper. "Dig and stitch mouse-ear roots on Friday during full moon, and wear 'em around your neck in a white silk."

"You're *crazy*," Charlie said.

"Teach you how to stop blood or make animals stand frozen or make blind horses see, all them things I'll teach you! Teach you to cure a swelled-up cow and unbewitch a goat. Show you how to make yourself invisible!"

"Oh," said Charlie.

Old Lady's heart beat like a Salvation tambourine.

The knob turned from the other side.

"You," said Charlie, "are funning me."

"No, I'm not," exclaimed Old Lady. "Oh, Charlie, why, I'll make you like a window, see right through you. Why, child, you'll be surprised!"

"Real invisible?"

"Real invisible!"

"You won't fetch onto me if I walk out?"

"Won't touch a bristle of you, son."

"Well," he drawled reluctantly, "all right."

The door opened. Charlie stood in his bare feet, head down, chin against chest. "Make me invisible," he said.

"First we got to catch us a bat," said Old Lady. "Start lookin'!"

She gave him some jerky beef for his hunger and watched him climb a tree. He went high up and high up and it was nice seeing him there and it was nice having him here and all about after so many years alone with nothing to say good morning to but bird-droppings and silvery snail tracks.

Pretty soon a bat with a broken wing fluttered down out of the tree. Old Lady snatched it up, beating warm and shrieking between its porcelain white teeth, and Charlie dropped down after it, hand upon clenched hand, yelling.

That night, with the moon nibbling at the spiced pine cones, Old Lady extracted a long silver needle from under her wide blue dress. Gumming her excitement and secret anticipation, she sighted up the dead bat and held the cold needle steady-steady.

She had long ago realized that her miracles, despite all perspirations and salts and sulphurs, failed. But she had

44

always dreamt that one day the miracles might start functioning, might spring up in crimson flowers and silver stars to prove that God had forgiven her for her pink body and her pink thoughts and her warm body and her warm thoughts as a young miss. But so far God had made no sign and said no word, but nobody knew this except Old Lady.

"Ready?" she asked Charlie, who crouched cross-kneed, wrapping his pretty legs in long goose-pimpled arms, his mouth open, making teeth. "Ready," he whispered, shivering.

"There!" She plunged the needle deep in the bat's right eye. "So!"

"Oh!" screamed Charlie, wadding up his face!

"Now I wrap it in gingham, and here, put it in your pocket, keep it there, bat and all. Go on!"

He pocketed the charm.

"Charlie!" she shrieked fearfully. "Charlie, where *are* you? I can't *see* you, child!"

"Here!" He jumped so the light ran in red streaks up his body. "I'm here, Old Lady!" He stared wildly at his arms, legs, chest, and toes. "I'm here!"

Her eyes looked as if they were watching a thousand fireflies crisscrossing each other in the wild night air.

"Charlie, oh, you went *fast*! Quick as a hummingbird! Oh, Charlie, come *back* to me!"

"But I'm *here*!" he wailed.

"Where?"

"By the fire, the fire! And—and I can see myself. I'm not invisible at all!"

Old Lady rocked on her lean flanks. "Course *you* can see *you*! Every invisible person knows himself. Otherwise, how could you eat, walk, or get around places? Charlie, touch me. Touch me so I *know* you."

Uneasily he put out a hand.

She pretended to jerk, startled, at his touch. "*Ah!*"

"You mean to say you can't *find* me?" he asked. "Truly?"

"Not the least half rump of you!"

She found a tree to stare at, and stared at it with shining eyes, careful not to glance at him. "Why, I sure *did* a trick *that* time!" She sighed with wonder. "Whooeee. Quickest invisible I *ever* made! Charlie. Charlie, how you *feel*?"

"Like creek water—all stirred."

"You'll settle."

Then after a pause she added, "Well, what you going to do now, Charlie, since you're invisible?"

All sorts of things shot through his brain, she could tell. Adventures stood up and danced like hell-fire in his eyes, and his mouth, just hanging, told what it meant to be a boy who imagined himself like the mountain winds. In a cold dream he

45

said, "I'll run across wheat fields, climb snow mountains, steal white chickens off'n farms. I'll kick pink pigs when they ain't looking. I'll pinch pretty girls' legs when they sleep, snap their garters in schoolrooms." Charlie looked at Old Lady, and from the shiny tips of her eyes she saw something wicked shape his face. "And other things I'll do, I'll do, I will," he said.

"Don't try nothing on me," warned Old Lady. "I'm brittle as spring ice and I don't take handling." Then: "What about your folks?"

"My folks?"

"You can't fetch yourself home looking like that. Scare the inside ribbons out of them. Your mother'd faint straight back like timber falling. Think they want you about the house to stumble over and your ma have to call you every three minutes, even though you're in the room next her elbow?"

Charlie had not considered it. He sort of simmered down and whispered out a little "Gosh" and felt of his long bones carefully.

"You'll be mighty lonesome. People looking through you like a water glass, people knocking you aside because they didn't reckon you to be underfoot. And women, Charlie, *women*——"

He swallowed. "What about women?"

"No woman will be giving you a second stare. And no woman wants to be kissed by a boy's mouth they can't even *find!*"

Charlie dug his bare toe in the soil contemplatively. He pouted. "Well, I'll stay invisible, anyway, for a spell. I'll have me some fun. I'll just be pretty careful, is all. I'll stay out from in front of wagons and horses and Pa. Pa shoots at the nariest sound." Charlie blinked. "Why, with me invisible, someday Pa might just up and fill me with buckshot, thinkin' I was a hill squirrel in the dooryard. Oh . . ."

Old Lady nodded at a tree. "That's likely."

"Well," he decided slowly, "I'll stay invisible for tonight, and tomorrow you can fix me back all whole again, Old Lady."

"Now if that ain't just like a critter, always wanting to be what he can't be," remarked Old Lady to a beetle on a log.

"What you mean?" said Charlie.

"Why," she explained, "it was real hard work, fixing you up. It'll take a little *time* for it to wear off. Like a coat of paint wears off, boy."

"You!" he cried. "You did this to me! Now you make me back, you make me seeable!"

"Hush," she said. "It'll wear off, a hand or a foot at a time."

"How'll it look, me around the hills with just one hand showing!"

"Like a five-winged bird hopping on the stones and bramble."

"Or a foot showing!"

"Like a small pink rabbit jumping thicket."

"Or my head floating!"

"Like a hairy balloon at the carnival!"

"How long before I'm *whole?*" he asked.

She deliberated that it might pretty well be an entire year.

He groaned. He began to sob and bite his lips and make fists. "You magicked me, you did this, you did this thing to me. Now I won't be able to run home!"

She winked. "But you *can* stay here, child, stay on with me real comfort-like, and I'll keep you fat and saucy."

He flung it out: "You did this on purpose! You mean old hag, you want to keep me here!"

He ran off through the shrubs on the instant.

"Charlie, come back!"

No answer but the pattern of his feet on the soft dark turf, and his wet choking cry which passed swiftly off and away.

She waited and then kindled herself a fire. "He'll be back," she whispered. And thinking inward on herself, she said, "And now I'll have me my company through spring and into late summer. Then, when I'm tired of him and want a silence, I'll send him home."

Charlie returned noiselessly with the first gray of dawn, gliding over the rimed turf to where Old Lady sprawled like a bleached stick before the scattered ashes.

He sat on some creek pebbles and stared at her.

She didn't dare look at him or beyond. He had made no sound, so how could she know he was anywhere about? She couldn't.

He sat there, tear marks on his cheeks.

Pretending to be just waking—but she had found no sleep from one end of the night to the other—Old Lady stood up, grunting and yawning, and turned in a circle to the dawn.

"Charlie?"

Her eyes passed from pines to soil, to sky, to the far hills. She called out his name, over and over again, and she felt like staring plumb straight at him, but she stopped herself. "Charlie? Oh, Charles!" she called, and heard the echoes say the very same.

He sat, beginning to grin a bit, suddenly, knowing he was close to her, yet she must feel alone. Perhaps he felt the growing of a secret power, perhaps he felt secure from the world, certainly he was *pleased* with his invisibility.

She said aloud, "Now where *can* that boy be? If he only made a noise so I could tell just where he is, maybe I'd fry him a breakfast."

She prepared the morning victuals, irritated at his continuous quiet. She sizzled bacon on a hickory stick. "The smell of it will draw his nose," she muttered.

While her back was turned he swiped all the frying bacon and devoured it hastily.

She whirled, crying out, "Lord!"

She eyed the clearing suspiciously. "Charlie, that *you?*"

Charlie wiped his mouth clean on his wrists.

She trotted about the clearing, making like she was trying to locate him. Finally, with a clever thought, acting blind, she headed straight for him, groping. "Charlie, where *are* you?"

A lightning streak, he evaded her, bobbing, ducking.

It took all her will power not to give chase; but you can't chase invisible boys, so she sat down, scowling, sputtering, and tried to fry more bacon. But every fresh strip she cut he would steal bubbling off the fire and run away far. Finally, cheeks burning, she cried, "I know where you are! Right *there!* I hear you run!" She pointed to one side of him, not too accurate. He ran again. "Now you're there!" she shouted. "There, and there!" pointing to all the places he was in the next five minutes. "I hear you press a grass blade, knock a flower, snap a twig. I got fine shell ears, delicate as roses. They can hear the stars moving!"

Silently he galloped off among the pines, his voice trailing back, "Can't hear me when I'm set on a rock. I'll just *set!*"

All day he sat on an observatory rock in the clear wind, motionless and sucking his tongue.

Old Lady gathered wood in the deep forest, feeling his eyes weaseling on her spine. She wanted to babble: "Oh, I see you, I see you! I was only fooling about invisible boys! You're right there!" But she swallowed her gall and gummed it tight.

The following morning he did the spiteful thing. He began leaping from behind trees. He made toad-faces, frog-faces, spider-faces at her, clenching down his lips with his fingers, popping his raw eyes, pushing up his nostrils so you could peer in and see his brain thinking.

Once she dropped her kindling. She pretended it was a blue jay startled her.

He made a motion as if to strangle her.

She trembled a little.

He made another move as if to bang her shins and spit on her cheek.

These motions she bore without a lid-flicker or a mouth-twitch.

He stuck out his tongue, making strange bad noises. He

wiggled his loose ears so she wanted to laugh, and finally she did laugh and explained it away quickly by saying, "Sat on a salamander! Whew, how it poked!"

By high noon the whole madness boiled to a terrible peak. For it was at that exact hour that Charlie came racing down the valley stark boy-naked!

Old Lady nearly fell flat with shock!

"Charlie!" she almost cried.

Charlie raced naked up one side of a hill and naked down the other—naked as day, naked as the moon, raw as the sun and a newborn chick, his feet shimmering and rushing like the wings of a low-skimming hummingbird.

Old Lady's tongue locked in her mouth. What could she say? Charlie, go dress? For *shame? Stop* that? *Could* she? Oh, Charlie, Charlie, God! Could she say that now? *Well?*

Upon the big rock, she witnessed him dancing up and down, naked as the day of his birth, stomping bare feet, smacking his hands on his knees and sucking in and out his white stomach like blowing and deflating a circus balloon.

She shut her eyes tight and prayed.

After three hours of this she pleaded, "Charlie, Charlie, come here! I got something to *tell* you!"

Like a fallen leaf he came, dressed again, praise the Lord.

"Charlie," she said, looking at the pine trees, "I see your right toe. *There* it is."

"You do?" he said.

"Yes," she said very sadly. "There it is like a horny toad on the grass. And there, up there's your left ear hanging on the air like a pink butterfly."

Charlie danced. "I'm forming in, I'm forming in!"

Old Lady nodded. "Here comes your ankle!"

"Gimme *both* my feet!" ordered Charlie.

"You got 'em."

"How about my hands?"

"I see one crawling on your knee like a daddy longlegs."

"How about the other one?"

"It's crawling too."

"I got a body?"

"Shaping up fine."

"I'll need my head to go home, Old Lady."

To go home, she thought wearily. "No!" she said, stubborn and angry. "No, you ain't got no head. No head at all," she cried. She'd leave that to the very last. "No head, no head," she insisted.

"No head?" he wailed.

"Yes, oh my God, yes, yes, you got your blamed head!" she snapped, giving up. "Now fetch me back my bat with the needle in his eye!"

49

He flung it at her. "Haaaa-yoooo!" His yelling went all up the valley, and long after he had run toward home she heard his echoes, racing.

Then she plucked up her kindling with a great dry weariness and started back toward her shack, sighing, talking. And Charlie followed her all the way, *really* invisible now, so she couldn't see him, just hear him, like a pine cone dropping or a deep underground stream trickling, or a squirrel clambering a bough; and over the fire at twilight she and Charlie sat, him so invisible, and her feeding him bacon he wouldn't take, so she ate it herself, and then she fixed some magic and fell asleep with Charlie, made out of sticks and rags and pebbles, but still warm and her very own son, slumbering and nice in her shaking mother arms . . . and they talked about golden things in drowsy voices until dawn made the fire slowly, slowly wither out. . . .

7

THE FLYING MACHINE

In the year a.d. 400, the Emperor Yuan held his throne by
the Great Wall of China, and the land was green with rain,
readying itself toward the harvest, at peace, the people in his
dominion neither too happy nor too sad.

Early on the morning of the first day of the first week of
the second month of the new year, the Emperor Yuan was
sipping tea and fanning himself against a warm breeze when
a servant ran across the scarlet and blue garden tiles, calling,
"Oh, Emperor, Emperor, a miracle!"

"Yes," said the Emperor, "the air *is* sweet this morning."

"No, no, a miracle!" said the servant, bowing quickly.

"And this tea is good in my mouth, surely that is a
miracle."

"No, no, Your Excellency."

"Let me guess then—the sun has risen and a new day is
upon us. Or the sea is blue. *That* now is the finest of all
miracles."

"Excellency, a man is flying!"

51

"What?" The Emperor stopped his fan.

"I saw him in the air, a man flying with wings. I heard a voice call out of the sky, and when I looked up, there he was, a dragon in the heavens with a man in its mouth, a dragon of paper and bamboo, colored like the sun and the grass."

"It is early," said the Emperor, "and you have just wakened from a dream."

"It is early, but I have seen what I have seen! Come, and you will see it too."

"Sit down with me here," said the Emperor. "Drink some tea. It must be a strange thing, if it is true, to see a man fly. You must have time to think of it, even as I must have time to prepare myself for the sight."

They drank tea.

"Please," said the servant at last, "or he will be gone."

The Emperor rose thoughtfully. "Now you may show me what you have seen."

They walked into a garden, across a meadow of grass, over a small bridge, through a grove of trees, and up a tiny hill.

"There!" said the servant.

The Emperor looked into the sky.

And in the sky, laughing so high that you could hardly hear him laugh, was a man; and the man was clothed in bright papers and reeds to make wings and a beautiful yellow tail, and he was soaring all about like the largest bird in a universe of birds, like a new dragon in a land of ancient dragons.

The man called down to them from high in the cool winds of morning. "I fly, I fly!"

The servant waved to him. "Yes, *yes!*"

The Emperor Yuan did not move. Instead he looked at the Great Wall of China now taking shape out of the farthest mist in the green hills, that splendid snake of stones which writhed with majesty across the entire land. That wonderful wall which had protected them for a timeless time from enemy hordes and preserved peace for years without number. He saw the town, nestled to itself by a river and a road and a hill, beginning to waken.

"Tell me," he said to his servant, "has anyone else seen this flying man?"

"I am the only one, Excellency," said the servant, smiling at the sky, waving.

The Emperor watched the heavens another minute and then said, "Call him down to me."

"Ho, come down, come down! The Emperor wishes to see you!" called the servant, hands cupped to his shouting mouth.

The Emperor glanced in all directions while the flying man

soared down the morning wind. He saw a farmer, early in his fields, watching the sky, and he noted where the farmer stood.

The flying man alit with a rustle of paper and a creak of bamboo reeds. He came proudly to the Emperor, clumsy in his rig, at last bowing before the old man.

"What have you done?" demanded the Emperor.

"I have flown in the sky, Your Excellency," replied the man.

"What *have* you done?" said the Emperor again.

"I have just told you!" cried the flier.

"You have told me nothing at all." The Emperor reached out a thin hand to touch the pretty paper and the birdlike keel of the apparatus. It smelled cool, of the wind.

"Is it not beautiful, Excellency?"

"Yes, too beautiful."

"It is the only one in the world!" smiled the man. "And I am the inventor."

"The *only* one in the world?"

"I swear it!"

"Who else knows of this?"

"No one. Not even my wife, who would think me mad with the sun. She thought I was making a kite. I rose in the night and walked to the cliffs far away. And when the morning breezes blew and the sun rose, I gathered my courage, Excellency, and leaped from the cliff. I flew! But my wife does not know of it."

"Well for her, then," said the Emperor. "Come along."

They walked back to the great house. The sun was full in the sky now, and the smell of the grass was refreshing. The Emperor, the servant, and the flier paused within the huge garden.

The Emperor clapped his hands. "Ho, guards!"

The guards came running.

"Hold this man."

The guards seized the flier.

"Call the executioner," said the Emperor.

"What's this!" cried the flier, bewildered. "What have I done?" He began to weep, so that the beautiful paper apparatus rustled.

"Here is the man who has made a certain machine," said the Emperor, "and yet asks us what he has created. He does not know himself. It is only necessary that he create, without knowing why he has done so, or what this thing will do."

The executioner came running with a sharp silver ax. He stood with his naked, large-muscled arms ready, his face covered with a serene white mask.

"One moment," said the Emperor. He turned to a near-by

53

table upon which sat a machine that he himself had created. The Emperor took a tiny golden key from his own neck. He fitted his key to the tiny, delicate machine and wound it up. Then he set the machine going.

The machine was a garden of metal and jewels. Set in motion, the birds sangs in tiny metal trees, wolves walked through miniature forests, and tiny people ran in and out of sun and shadow, fanning themselves with miniature fans, listening to tiny emerald birds, and standing by impossibly small but tinkling fountains.

"Is *it* not beautiful?" said the Emperor. "If you asked me what I have done here, I could answer you well. I have made birds sing, I have made forests murmur, I have set people to walking in this woodland, enjoying the leaves and shadows and songs. That is what I have done."

"But, oh, Emperor!" pleaded the flier, on his knees, the tears pouring down his face. "I have done a similar thing! I have found beauty. I have flown on the morning wind. I have looked down on all the sleeping houses and gardens. I have smelled the sea and even *seen* it, beyond the hills, from my high place. And I have soared like a bird; oh, I cannot say how beautiful it is up there, in the sky, with the wind about me, the wind blowing me here like a feather, there like a fan, the way the sky smells in the morning! And how free one feels! *That* is beautiful, Emperor, that is beautiful too!"

"Yes," said the Emperor sadly, "I know it must be true. For I felt my heart move with you in the air and I wondered: What is it like? How does it feel? How do the distant pools look from so high? And how my houses and servants? Like ants? And how the distant towns not yet awake?"

"Then spare me!"

"But there are times," said the Emperor, more sadly still, "when one must lose a little beauty if one is to keep what little beauty one already has. I do not fear you, yourself, but I fear another man."

"What man?"

"Some other man who, seeing you, will build a thing of bright papers and bamboo like this. But the other man will have an evil face and an evil heart, and the beauty will be gone. It is this man I fear."

"Why? Why?"

"Who is to say that someday just such a man, in just such an apparatus of paper and reed, might not fly in the sky and drop huge stones upon the Great Wall of China?" said the Emperor.

No one moved or said a word.

"Off with his head," said the Emperor.

The executioner whirled his silver ax.

"Burn the kite and the inventor's body and bury their ashes together," said the Emperor.

The servants retreated to obey.

The Emperor turned to his hand-servant, who had seen the man flying. "Hold your tongue. It was all a dream, a most sorrowful and beautiful dream. And that farmer in the distant field who also saw, tell him it would pay him to consider it only a vision. If ever the word passes around, you and the farmer die within the hour."

"You are merciful, Emperor."

"No, not merciful," said the old man. Beyond the garden wall he saw the guards burning the beautiful machine of paper and reeds that smelled of the morning wind. He saw the dark smoke climb into the sky. "No, only very much bewildered and afraid." He saw the guards digging a tiny pit wherein to bury the ashes. "What is the life of one man against those of a million others? I must take solace from that thought."

He took the key from its chain about his neck and once more wound up the beautiful miniature garden. He stood looking out across the land at the Great Wall, the peaceful town, the green fields, the rivers and streams. He sighed. The tiny garden whirred its hidden and delicate machinery and set itself in motion; tiny people walked in forests, tiny faces loped through sun-speckled glades in beautiful shining pelts, and among the tiny trees flew little bits of high song and bright blue and yellow color, flying, flying, flying in that small sky.

"Oh," said the Emperor, closing his eyes, "look at the birds, look at the birds!"

8

THE MURDERER

MUSIC MOVED with him in the white halls. He passed an office door: "The Merry Widow Waltz." Another door: "Afternoon of a Faun." A third: "Kiss Me Again." He turned into a cross corridor: "The Sword Dance" buried him in cymbals, drums, pots, pans, knives, forks, thunder, and tin lightning. All washed away as he hurried through an anteroom where a secretary sat nicely stunned by Beethoven's Fifth. He moved himself before her eyes like a hand; she didn't see him.

His wrist radio buzzed.

"Yes?"

"This is Lee, Dad. Don't forget about my allowance."

"Yes, son, yes. I'm busy."

"Just didn't want you to forget, Dad," said the wrist radio. Tchaikovsky's "Romeo and Juliet" swarmed about the voice and flushed into the long halls.

The psychiatrist moved in the beehive of offices, in the cross-pollination of themes, Stravinsky mating with Bach, Haydn unsuccessfully repulsing Rachmaninoff, Schubert slain by Duke Ellington. He nodded to the humming secretaries and the whistling doctors fresh to their morning work. At his office he checked a few papers with his stenographer, who sang under her breath, then phoned the police captain upstairs. A few minutes later a red light blinked, a voice said from the ceiling:

"Prisoner delivered to Interview Chamber Nine."

He unlocked the chamber door, stepped in, heard the door lock behind him.

"Go away," said the prisoner, smiling.

The psychiatrist was shocked by that smile. A very sunny, pleasant warm thing, a thing that shed bright light upon the room. Dawn among the dark hills. High noon at midnight, that smile. The blue eyes sparkled serenely above that display of self-assured dentistry.

"I'm here to help you," said the psychiatrist, frowning. Something was wrong with the room. He had hesitated the moment he entered. He glanced around. The prisoner laughed. "If you're wondering why it's so quiet in here, I just kicked the radio to death."

Violent, thought the doctor.

The prisoner read this thought, smiled, put out a gentle hand. "No, only to machines that yak-yak-yak."

Bits of the wall radio's tubes and wires lay on the gray carpeting. Ignoring these, feeling that smile upon him like a heat lamp, the psychiatrist sat across from his patient in the unusual silence which was like the gathering of a storm.

"You're Mr. Albert Brock, who calls himself The Murderer?"

Brock nodded pleasantly. "Before we start . . ." He moved quietly and quickly to detach the wrist radio from the doctor's arm. He tucked it in his teeth like a walnut, gritted and heard it crack, handed it back to the appalled psychiatrist as if he had done them both a favor. "That's better."

The psychiatrist stared at the ruined machine. "You're running up quite a damage bill."

"I don't care," smiled the patient. "As the old song goes: 'Don't Care What Happens to Me!' " He hummed it.

The psychiatrist said: "Shall we start?"

"Fine. The first victim, or one of the first, was my telephone. Murder most foul. I shoved it in the kitchen Insinkerator! Stopped the disposal unit in mid-swallow. Poor thing strangled to death. After that I shot the television set!"

The psychiatrist said, "Mmm."

"Fired six shots right through the cathode. Made a beautiful tinkling crash, like a dropped chandelier."

"Nice imagery."

"Thanks, I always dreamt of being a writer."

57

"Suppose you tell me when you first began to hate the telephone."

"It frightened me as a child. Uncle of mine called it the Ghost Machine. Voices without bodies. Scared the living hell out of me. Later in life I was never comfortable. Seemed to me a phone was an impersonal instrument. If it *felt* like it, it let your personality go through its wires. If it didn't *want* to, it just drained your personality away until what slipped through at the other end was some cold fish of a voice all steel, copper, plastic, no warmth, no reality. It's easy to say the wrong thing on telephones; the telephone changes your meaning on you. First thing you know, you've made an enemy. Then, of course, the telephone's such a *convenient* thing; it just sits there and *demands* you call someone who doesn't want to be called. Friends were always calling, calling, calling me. Hell, I hadn't any time of my own. When it wasn't the telephone it was the television, the radio, the phonograph. When it wasn't the television or radio or the phonograph it was motion pictures at the corner theater, motion pictures projected, with commercials on low-lying cumulus clouds. It doesn't rain rain any more, it rains soapsuds. When it wasn't High-Fly Cloud advertisements, it was music by Mozzek in every restaurant; music and commercials on the busses I rode to work. When it wasn't music, it was inter-office communications, and my horror chamber of a radio wrist watch on which my friends and my wife phoned every five minutes. What is there about such 'conveniences' that makes them so *temptingly* convenient? The average man thinks, Here I am, time on my hands, and there on my wrist is a wrist telephone, so why not just buzz old Joe up, eh? 'Hello, hello!' I love my friends, my wife, humanity, very much, but when one minute my wife calls to say, 'Where are you *now*, dear?' and a friend calls and says, 'Got the best off-color joke to tell you. Seems there was a guy——' And a stranger calls and cries out, 'This is the Find-Fax Poll. What gum are you chewing at this very *instant!*' Well!"

"How did you feel during the week?"

"The fuse lit. On the edge of the cliff. That same afternoon I did what I did at the office."

"Which was?"

"I poured a paper cup of water into the intercommunications system."

The psychiatrist wrote on his pad.

"And the system shorted?"

"Beautifully! The Fourth of July on wheels! My God, stenographers ran around looking *lost!* What an uproar!"

"Felt better temporarily, eh?"

"Fine! Then I got the idea at noon of stomping my wrist

radio on the sidewalk. A shrill voice was just yelling out of it at me, 'This is People's Poll Number Nine. What did you eat for lunch?' when I kicked the Jesus out of the wrist radio!"

"Felt even *better*, eh?"

"It *grew* on me!" Brock rubbed his hands together. "Why didn't I start a solitary revolution, deliver man from certain 'conveniences'? 'Convenient for who?' I cried. Convenient for friends: 'Hey, Al, thought I'd call you from the locker room out here at Green Hills. Just made a sockdolager hole in one! A hole in one, Al! A *beautiful* day. Having a shot of whiskey now. Thought you'd want to know, Al!' Convenient for my office, so when I'm in the field with my radio car there's no moment when I'm not in touch. In *touch!* There's a slimy phrase. Touch, hell. *Gripped!* Pawed, rather. Mauled and massaged and pounded by FM voices. You can't leave your car without checking in: 'Have stopped to visit gas-station men's room.' 'Okay, Brock, step on it!' 'Brock, what *took* you so long?' 'Sorry, sir.' 'Watch it next time, Brock.' '*Yes, sir!*' So, do you know what I did, Doctor? I bought a quart of French chocolate ice cream and spooned it into the car radio transmitter."

"Was there any *special* reason for selecting French chocolate ice cream to spoon into the broadcasting unit?"

Brock thought about it and smiled. "It's my favorite flavor."

"Oh," said the doctor.

"I figured, hell, what's good enough for me is good enough for the radio transmitter."

"What made you think of spooning *ice cream* into the radio?"

"It was a hot day."

The doctor paused.

"And what happened next?"

"Silence happened next. God, it was *beautiful*. That car radio cackling all day, Brock go here, Brock go there, Brock check in, Brock check out, okay Brock, hour lunch, Brock, lunch over, Brock, Brock, Brock. Well, that silence was like putting ice cream in my ears."

"You seem to like ice cream a lot."

"I just rode around feeling of the silence. It's a big bolt of the nicest, softest flannel ever made. Silence. A whole hour of it. I just sat in my car; smiling, feeling of that flannel with my ears. I felt *drunk* with Freedom!"

"Go on."

"Then I got the idea of the portable diathermy machine. I rented one, took it on the bus going home that night. There sat all the tired commuters with their wrist radios, talking to their wives, saying, 'Now I'm at Forty-third, now

I'm at Forty-fourth, here I am at Forty-ninth, now turning at Sixty-first.' One husband cursing, 'Well, get *out* of that bar, damn it, and get home and get dinner started, I'm at Seventieth!' And the transit-system radio playing 'Tales from the Vienna Woods,' a canary singing words about a first-rate wheat cereal. Then—I switched on my diathermy! Static! Interference! All wives cut off from husbands grousing about a hard day at the office. All husbands cut off from wives who had just seen their children break a window! The 'Vienna Woods' chopped down, the canary mangled! *Silence!* A terrible, unexpected silence. The bus inhabitants faced with having to converse with each other. Panic! Sheer, animal panic!"

"The police seized you?"

"The bus *had* to stop. After all, the music *was* being scrambled, husbands and wives *were* out of touch with reality. Pandemonium, riot, and chaos. Squirrels chattering in cages! A trouble unit arrived, triangulated on me instantly, had me reprimanded, fined, and home, minus my diathermy machine, in jig time."

"Mr. Brock, may I suggest that so far your whole pattern here is not very—practical? If you didn't like transit radios or office radios or car business radios, why didn't you join a fraternity of radio haters, start petitions, get legal and constitutional rulings? After all, this *is* a democracy."

"And I," said Brock, "am that thing called a minority. I *did* join fraternities, picket, pass petitions, take it to court. Year after year I protested. Everyone laughed. Everyone else *loved* bus radios and commercials. *I* was out of step."

"Then you should have taken it like a good soldier, don't you think? The majority rules."

"But they went too far. If a little music and 'keeping in touch' was charming, they figured a lot would be ten times as charming. I went *wild!* I got home to find my wife hysterical. *Why?* Because she had been completely out of touch with me for half a day. Remember, I did a dance on my wrist radio? Well, that night I laid plans to murder my house."

"Are you *sure* that's how you want me to write it down?"

"That's semantically accurate. Kill it dead. It's one of those talking, singing, humming, weather-reporting, poetry-reading, novel-reciting, jingle-jangling, rockaby-crooning-when-you-go-to-bed houses. A house that screams opera to you in the shower and teaches you Spanish in your sleep. One of those blathering caves where all kinds of electronic Oracles make you feel a trifle larger than a thimble, with stoves that say, 'I'm apricot pie, and I'm *done*,' or 'I'm prime roast beef, so *baste* me!' and other nursery gibberish like that.

60

With beds that rock you to sleep and *shake* you awake. A house that *barely* tolerates humans, I tell you. A front door that barks: 'You've mud on your feet, sir!' And an electronic vacuum hound that snuffles around after you from room to room, inhaling every fingernail or ash you drop. Jesus God, *I* say, Jesus God!"

"Quietly," suggested the psychiatrist.

"Remember that Gilbert and Sullivan song—'I've Got It on My List, It Never Will Be Missed'? All night I listed grievances. Next morning early I bought a pistol. I *purposely* muddied my feet. I stood at our front door. The front door shrilled, 'Dirty feet, muddy feet! Wipe your feet! Please be *neat!*' I shot the damn thing in its keyhole. I ran to the kitchen, where the stove was just whining, 'Turn me *over!*' In the middle of a mechanical omelet I did the stove to death. Oh, how it sizzled and screamed, 'I'm *shorted!*' Then the telephone rang like a spoiled brat. I shoved it down the Insinkerator. I must state here and now I have *nothing* whatever against the Insinkerator; it was an innocent bystander. I feel sorry for it now, a practical device indeed, which never said a word, purred like a sleepy lion most of the time, and digested our leftovers. I'll have it restored. Then I went in and shot the televisor, that insidious beast, that Medusa, which freezes a billion people to stone every night, staring fixedly, that Siren which called and sang and promised so much and gave, after all, so little, but myself always going back, going back, hoping and waiting until—bang! Like a headless turkey, gobbling, my wife whooped out the front door. The police came. Here I *am!*"

He sat back happily and lit a cigarette.

"And did you realize, in committing these crimes, that the wrist radio, the broadcasting transmitter, the phone, the bus radio, the office intercoms, all were rented or were someone else's property?"

"I would do it all over again, so help me God."

The psychiatrist sat there in the sunshine of that beatific smile.

"You don't want any further help from the Office of Mental Health? You're ready to take the consequences?"

"This is only the beginning," said Mr. Brock. "I'm the vanguard of the small public which is tired of noise and being taken advantage of and pushed around and yelled at, every moment music, every moment in touch with some voice somewhere, do this, do that, quick, quick, now here, now there. You'll see. The revolt begins. My name will go down in history!"

"Mmm." The psychiatrist seemed to be thinking.

"It'll take time, of course. It was all so enchanting at

61

first. The very *idea* of these things, the practical uses, was wonderful. They were almost toys, to be played with, but the people got too involved, went too far, and got wrapped up in a pattern of social behavior and couldn't get out, couldn't admit they were *in*, even. So they rationalized their nerves as something else. 'Our modern age,' they said. 'Conditions,' they said. 'High-strung,' they said. But mark my words, the seed has been sown. I got world-wide coverage on TV, radio, films; *there's* an irony for you. That was five days ago. A billion people know about me. Check your financial columns. Any day now. Maybe today. Watch for a sudden spurt, a rise in sales for French chocolate ice cream!"

"I see," said the psychiatrist.

"Can I go back to my nice private cell now, where I can be alone and quiet for six months?"

"Yes," said the psychiatrist quietly.

"Don't worry about me," said Mr. Brock, rising. "I'm just going to sit around for a long time stuffing that nice soft bolt of quiet material in both ears."

"Mmm," said the psychiatrist, going to the door.

"Cheers," said Mr. Brock.

"Yes," said the psychiatrist.

He pressed a code signal on a hidden button, the door opened, he stepped out, the door shut and locked. Alone, he moved in the offices and corridors. The first twenty yards of his walk were accompanied by "Tambourine Chinois." Then it was "Tzigane," Bach's Passacaglia and Fugue in something Minor, "Tiger Rag," "Love Is Like a Cigarette." He took his broken wrist radio from his pocket like a dead praying mantis. He turned in at his office. A bell sounded; a voice came out of the ceiling, "Doctor?"

"Just finished with Brock," said the psychiatrist.

"Diagnosis?"

"Seems completely disorientated, but convivial. Refuses to accept the simplest realities of his environment and work *with* them."

"Prognosis?"

"Indefinite. Left him enjoying a piece of invisible material."

Three phones rang. A duplicate wrist radio in his desk drawer buzzed like a wounded grasshopper. The intercom flashed a pink light and click-clicked. Three phones rang. The drawer buzzed. Music blew in through the open door. The psychiatrist, humming quietly, fitted the new wrist radio to his wrist, flipped the intercom, talked a moment, picked up one telephone, talked, picked up another telephone, talked, picked up the third telephone, talked, touched the wrist-radio button, talked calmly and quietly, his face cool and serene, in the middle of the music and the lights flashing, the two phones ringing again, and his hands moving, and his wrist radio buzzing, and the intercoms talking, and voices speaking from the ceiling. And he went on quietly this way through the remainder of a cool, air-conditioned, and long afternoon; telephone, wrist radio, intercom, telephone, wrist radio, intercom, telephone, wrist radio, intercom, telephone, wrist radio, intercom, telephone, wrist radio, intercom, telephone, wrist radio . . .

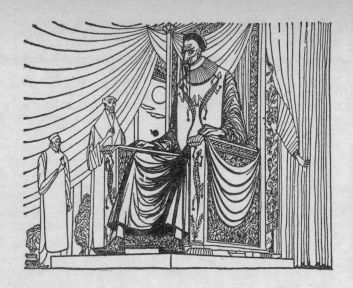

9

THE GOLDEN KITE, THE SILVER WIND

"IN THE SHAPE of a *pig?*" cried the Mandarin.

"In the shape of a pig," said the messenger, and departed.

"Oh, what an evil day in an evil year," cried the Mandarin. "The town of Kwan-Si, beyond the hill, was very small in my childhood. Now it has grown so large that at last they are building a wall."

"But why should a wall two miles away make my good father sad and angry all within the hour?" asked his daughter quietly.

"They build their wall," said the Mandarin, "in the shape of a pig! Do you see? Our own city wall is built in the shape of an orange. That pig will devour us, greedily!"

"Ah."

They both sat thinking.

Life was full of symbols and omens. Demons lurked everywhere, Death swam in the wetness of an eye, the turn of a gull's wing meant rain, a fan held *so*, the tilt of a roof, and, yes, even a city wall was of immense importance. Travelers and tourists, caravans, musicians, artists, coming upon these two towns, equally judging the portents, would say, "The city shaped like an orange? No! I will enter the city shaped like a pig and prosper, eating all, growing fat with good luck and prosperity!"

The Mandarin wept. "All is lost! These symbols and signs terrify. Our city will come on evil days."

"Then," said the daughter, "call in your stonemasons and temple builders. I will whisper from behind the silken screen and you will know the words."

The old man clapped his hands despairingly. "Ho, stonemasons! Ho, builders of towns and palaces!"

The men who knew marble and granite and onyx and quartz came quickly. The Mandarin faced them most uneasily, himself waiting for a whisper from the silken screen behind his throne. At last the whisper came.

"I have called you here," said the whisper.

"I have called you here," said the Mandarin aloud, "because our city is shaped like an orange, and the vile city of Kwan-Si has this day shaped theirs like a ravenous pig——"

Here the stonemasons groaned and wept. Death rattled his cane in the outer courtyard. Poverty made a sound like a wet cough in the shadows of the room.

"And so," said the whisper, said the Mandarin, "you raisers of walls must go bearing trowels and rocks and change the shape of *our* city!"

The architects and masons gasped. The Mandarin himself gasped at what he had said. The whisper whispered. The Mandarin went on: "And you will change our walls into a club which may beat the pig and drive it off!"

The stonemasons rose up, shouting. Even the Mandarin, delighted at the words from his mouth, applauded, stood down from his throne. "Quick!" he cried. "To work!"

When his men had gone, smiling and bustling, the Mandarin turned with great love to the silken screen. "Daughter," he whispered, "I will embrace you." There was no reply. He stepped around the screen, and she was gone.

Such modesty, he thought. She has slipped away and left me with a triumph, as if it were mine.

The news spread through the city; the Mandarin was acclaimed. Everyone carried stone to the walls. Fireworks were set off and the demons of death and poverty did not linger, as all worked together. At the end of the month the wall had been changed. It was now a mighty bludgeon with which to drive pigs, boars, even lions, far away. The Mandarin slept like a happy fox every night.

"I would like to see the Mandarin of Kwan-Si when the news is learned. Such pandemonium and hysteria; he will likely throw himself from a mountain! A little more of that wine, oh Daughter-who-thinks-like-a-son."

But the pleasure was like a winter flower; it died swiftly. That very afternoon the messenger rushed into the court-room. "Oh, Mandarin, disease, early sorrow, avalanches, grasshopper plagues, and poisoned well water!"

The Mandarin trembled.

"The town of Kwan-Si," said the messenger, "which was built like a pig and which animal we drove away by changing our walls to a mighty stick, has now turned triumph to winter ashes. They have built their city's walls like a great bonfire to burn our stick!"

The Mandarin's heart sickened within him, like an autumn fruit upon an ancient tree. "Oh, gods! Travelers will spurn us. Tradesmen, reading the symbols, will turn from the stick, so easily destroyed, to the fire, which conquers all!"

"No," said a whisper like a snowflake from behind the silken screen.

"No," said the startled Mandarin.

"Tell my stonemasons," said the whisper that was a falling drop of rain, "to build our walls in the shape of a shining lake."

The Mandarin said this aloud, his heart warmed.

"And with this lake of water," said the whisper and the old man, "we will quench the fire and put it out forever!"

The city turned out in joy to learn that once again they had been saved by the magnificent Emperor of ideas. They ran to the walls and built them nearer to this new vision, singing, not as loudly as before, of course, for they were tired, and not as quickly, for since it had taken a month to build the wall the first time, they had had to neglect business and crops and therefore were somewhat weaker and poorer.

There then followed a succession of horrible and wonderful days, one in another like a nest of frightening boxes.

"Oh, Emperor," cried the messenger, "Kwan-Si has re-built their walls to resemble a mouth with which to drink all our lake!"

"Then," said the Emperor, standing very close to his silken screen, "build our walls like a needle to sew up that mouth!"

"Emperor!" screamed the messenger. "They make their walls like a sword to break your needle!"

The Emperor held, trembling, to the silken screen. "Then shift the stones to form a scabbard to sheathe that sword!"

"Mercy," wept the messenger the following morn, "they

have worked all night and shaped their walls like lightning which will explode and destroy that sheath!"

Sickness spread in the city like a pack of evil dogs. Shops closed. The population, working now steadily for endless months upon the changing of the walls, resembled Death himself, clattering his white bones like musical instruments in the wind. Funerals began to appear in the streets, though it was the middle of summer, a time when all should be tending and harvesting. The Mandarin fell so ill that he had his bed drawn up by the silken screen and there he lay, miserably giving his architectural orders. The voice behind the screen was weak now, too, and faint, like the wind in the eaves.

"Kwan-Si is an eagle. Then our walls must be a net for that eagle. They are a sun to burn our net. Then we build a moon to eclipse their sun!"

Like a rusted machine, the city ground to a halt.

At last the whisper behind the screen cried out:

"In the name of the gods, send for Kwan-Si!"

Upon the last day of summer the Mandarin Kwan-Si, very ill and withered away, was carried into our Mandarin's courtroom by four starving footmen. The two mandarins were propped up, facing each other. Their breaths fluttered like winter winds in their mouths. A voice said:

"Let us put an end to this."

The old men nodded.

"This cannot go on," said the faint voice. "Our people do nothing but rebuild our cities to a different shape every day, every hour. They have no time to hunt, to fish, to love, to be good to their ancestors and their ancestors' children."

"This I admit," said the mandarins of the towns of the Cage, the Moon, the Spear, the Fire, the Sword and this, that, and other things.

"Carry us into the sunlight," said the voice.

The old men were borne out under the sun and up a little hill. In the late summer breeze a few very thin children were flying dragon kites in all the colors of the sun, and frogs and grass, the color of the sea and the color of coins and wheat.

The first Mandarin's daughter stood by his bed.

"See," she said.

"Those are nothing but kites," said the two old men.

"But what is a kite on the ground?" she said. "It is nothing. What does it need to sustain it and make it beautiful and truly spiritual?"

"The wind, of course!" said the others.

"And what do the sky and the wind need to make *them* beautiful?"

"A kite, of course—many kites, to break the monotony, the sameness of the sky. Colored kites, flying!"

"So," said the Mandarin's daughter. "You, Kwan-Si, will make a last rebuilding of your town to resemble nothing more nor less than the wind. And we shall build like a golden kite. The wind will beautify the kite and carry it to wondrous heights. And the kite will break the sameness of the wind's existence and give it purpose and meaning. One without the other is nothing. Together, all will be beauty and co-operation and a long and enduring life."

Whereupon the two mandarins were so overjoyed that they took their first nourishment in days, momentarily were given strength, embraced, and lavished praise upon each other, called the Mandarin's daughter a boy, a man, a stone pillar, a warrior, and a true and unforgettable son. Almost immediately they parted and hurried to their towns, calling out and singing, weakly but happily.

And so, in time, the towns became the Town of the Golden Kite and the Town of the Silver Wind. And harvestings were harvested and business tended again, and the flesh returned, and disease ran off like a frightened jackal. And on every night of the year the inhabitants in the Town of the Kite could hear the good clear wind sustaining them. And those in the Town of the Wind could hear the kite singing, whispering, rising, and beautifying them.

"So be it," said the Mandarin in front of his silken screen.

10

I SEE YOU NEVER

THE SOFT KNOCK came at the kitchen door, and when Mrs. O'Brian opened it, there on the back porch were her best tenant, Mr. Ramirez, and two police officers, one on each side of him. Mr. Ramirez just stood there, walled in and small.

"Why, Mr. Ramirez!" said Mrs. O'Brian.

Mr. Ramirez was overcome. He did not seem to have words to explain.

He had arrived at Mrs. O'Brian's rooming house more than two years earlier and had lived there ever since. He had come by bus from Mexico City to San Diego and had then gone up to Los Angeles. There he had found the clean little room, with glossy blue linoleum, and pictures and calendars on the flowered walls, and Mrs. O'Brian as the strict but kindly landlady. During the war he had worked at the airplane factory and made parts for the planes that flew off somewhere, and even now, after the war, he still held his job. From the first he had made big money. He saved some of it, and he got drunk only once a week—a privilege that, to Mrs. O'Brian's way of thinking, every good workingman deserved, unquestioned and unreprimanded.

Inside Mrs. O'Brian's kitchen, pies were baking in the oven. Soon the pies would come out with complexions like Mr. Ramirez'—brown and shiny and crisp, with slits in them for the air almost like the slits of Mr. Ramirez' dark eyes. The kitchen smelled good. The policemen leaned forward, lured by the odor. Mr. Ramirez gazed at his feet as if they had carried him into all this trouble.

"What happened, Mr. Ramirez?" asked Mrs. O'Brian.

Behind Mrs. O'Brian, as he lifted his eyes, Mr. Ramirez saw the long table laid with clean white linen and set with a platter, cool, shining glasses, a water pitcher with ice cubes floating inside it, a bowl of fresh potato salad and one of bananas and oranges, cubed and sugared. At this table sat Mrs. O'Brian's children—her three grown sons, eating and conversing, and her two younger daughters, who were staring at the policemen as they ate.

"I have been here thirty months," said Mr. Ramirez quietly, looking at Mrs. O'Brian's plump hands.

"That's six months too long," said one policeman. "He only had a temporary visa. We've just got around to looking for him."

Soon after Mr. Ramirez had arrived he bought a radio for his little room; evenings, he turned it up very loud and enjoyed it. And he had bought a wrist watch and enjoyed that too. And on many nights he had walked silent streets and seen the bright clothes in the windows and bought some of them, and he had seen the jewels and bought some of them for his few lady friends. And he had gone to picture shows five nights a week for a while. Then, also, he had ridden the streetcars—all night some nights—smelling the electricity, his dark eyes moving over the advertisements, feeling the wheels rumble under him, watching the little sleeping houses and big hotels slip by. Besides that, he had gone to large restaurants, where he had eaten many-course dinners, and to the opera and the theater. And he had bought a car, which later, when he forgot to pay for it, the dealer had driven off angrily from in front of the rooming house.

"So here I am," said Mr. Ramirez now, "to tell you I must give up my room, Mrs. O'Brian. I come to get my baggage and clothes and go with these men."

"Back to Mexico?"

"Yes. To Lagos. That is a little town north of Mexico City."

"I'm sorry, Mr. Ramirez."

"I'm packed," said Mr. Ramirez hoarsely, blinking his dark eyes rapidly and moving his hands helplessly before him. The policemen did not touch him. There was no necessity for that.

"Here is the key, Mrs. O'Brian," Mr. Ramirez said. "I have my bag already."

Mrs. O'Brian, for the first time, noticed a suitcase standing behind him on the porch.

Mr. Ramirez looked in again at the huge kitchen, at the bright silver cutlery and the young people eating and the shining waxed floor. He turned and looked for a long moment at the apartment house next door, rising up three stories, high and beautiful. He looked at the balconies and fire escapes and back-porch stairs, at the lines of laundry snapping in the wind.

"You've been a good tenant," said Mrs. O'Brian.

"Thank you, thank you, Mrs. O'Brian," he said softly. He closed his eyes.

Mrs. O'Brian stood holding the door half open. One of her sons, behind her, said that her dinner was getting cold, but she shook her head at him and turned back to Mr. Ramirez. She remembered a visit she had once made to some Mexican border towns—the hot days, the endless crickets leaping and falling or lying dead and brittle like the small cigars in the shop windows, and the canals taking river water out to the farms, the dirt roads, the scorched scape. She remembered the silent towns, the warm beer, the hot, thick foods each day. She remembered the slow, dragging horses and the parched jack rabbits on the road. She remembered the iron mountains and the dusty valleys and the ocean beaches that spread hundreds of miles with no sound but the waves—no cars, no buildings, nothing.

"I'm sure sorry, Mr. Ramirez," she said.

"I don't want to go back, Mrs. O'Brian," he said weakly. "I like it here, I want to stay here. I've worked, I've got money. I look all right, don't I? And I don't want to go back!"

"I'm sorry, Mr. Ramirez," she said. "I wish there was something I could do."

"Mrs. O'Brian!" he cried suddenly, tears rolling out from under his eyelids. He reached out his hand and took her hand fervently, shaking it, wringing it, holding to it. "Mrs. O'Brian, I see you never, I see you never!"

The policemen smiled at this, but Mr. Ramirez did not notice it, and they stopped smiling very soon.

"Good-by, Mrs. O'Brian. You have been good to me. Oh, good-by, Mrs. O'Brian. I see you never!"

The policemen waited for Mr. Ramirez to turn, pick up his

suitcase, and walk away. Then they followed him, tipping their caps to Mrs. O'Brian. She watched them go down the porch steps. Then she shut the door quietly and went slowly back to her chair at the table. She pulled the chair out and sat down. She picked up the shining knife and fork and started once more upon her steak.

"Hurry up, Mom," said one of the sons. "It'll be cold."

Mrs. O'Brian took one bite and chewed on it for a long, slow time; then she stared at the closed door. She laid down her knife and fork.

"What's wrong, Ma?" asked her son.

"I just realized," said Mrs. O'Brian—she put her hand to her face—"I'll never see Mr. Ramirez again."

11

EMBROIDERY

THE DARK porch air in the late afternoon was full of needle flashes, like a movement of gathered silver insects in the light. The three women's mouths twitched over their work. Their bodies lay back and then imperceptibly forward, so that the rocking chairs tilted and murmured. Each woman looked to her own hands, as if quite suddenly she had found her heart beating there.

"What time is it?"

"Ten minutes to five."

"Got to get up in a minute and shell those peas for dinner."

"But——" said one of them.

"Oh yes, I forgot. How foolish of me. . . ." The first woman paused, put down her embroidery and needle, and looked through the open porch door, through the warm interior of the quiet house, to the silent kitchen. There upon the table, seeming more like symbols of domesticity than anything she had ever seen in her life, lay the mound of fresh-washed peas in their neat, resilient jackets, waiting for her fingers to bring them into the world.

"Go hull them if it'll make you feel good," said the second woman.

"No," said the first. "I won't. I just won't."

The third woman sighed. She embroidered a rose, a leaf, a daisy on a green field. The embroidery needle rose and vanished.

The second woman was working on the finest, most delicate piece of embroidery of them all, deftly poking, finding, and returning the quick needle upon innumerable journeys. Her quick black glance was on each motion. A flower, a man, a road, a sun, a house; the scene grew under hand, a miniature beauty, perfect in every threaded detail.

"It seems at times like this that it's always your hands you turn to," she said, and the others nodded enough to make the rockers rock again.

"I believe," said the first lady, "that our souls are in our hands. For we do *everything* to the world with our hands. Sometimes I think we don't use our hands half enough; it's certain we don't use our heads."

They all peered more intently at what their hands were doing. "Yes," said the third lady, "when you look back on a whole lifetime, it seems you don't remember faces so much as hands and what they did."

They recounted to themselves the lids they had lifted, the doors they had opened and shut, the flowers they had picked, the dinners they had made, all with slow or quick fingers, as was their manner or custom. Looking back, you saw a flurry of hands, like a magician's dream, doors popping wide, taps turned, brooms wielded, children spanked. The flutter of pink hands was the only sound; the rest was a dream without voices.

"No supper to fix tonight or tomorrow night or the next night after that," said the third lady.

"No windows to open or shut."

"No coal to shovel in the basement furnace next winter."

"No papers to clip cooking articles out of."

And suddenly they were crying. The tears rolled softly down their faces and fell into the material upon which their fingers twitched.

"This won't help things," said the first lady at last, putting the back of her thumb to each under-eyelid. She looked at her thumb and it was wet.

"Now look what I've done!" cried the second lady, exasperated. The others stopped and peered over. The second lady held out her embroidery. There was the scene, perfect except that while the embroidered yellow sun shone down upon the embroidered green field, and the embroidered brown road curved toward an embroidered pink house, the man standing on the road had something wrong with his face.

"I'll just have to rip out the whole pattern, practically, to fix it right," said the second lady.

"What a shame." They all stared intently at the beautiful scene with the flaw in it.

The second lady began to pick away at the thread with her little deft scissors flashing. The pattern came out thread by thread. She pulled and yanked, almost viciously. The man's face was gone. She continued to seize at the threads.

"What are you *doing?*" asked the other woman.

They leaned and saw what she had done.

The man was gone from the road. She had taken him out entirely.

They said nothing but returned to their own tasks.

"What time is it?" asked someone.

"Five minutes to five."

"Is it supposed to happen at five o'clock?"

"Yes."

"And they're not sure what it'll do to anything, really, when it happens?"

"No, not sure."

"Why didn't we stop them before it got this far and this big?"

"It's twice as big as ever before. No, ten times, maybe a thousand."

"This isn't like the first one or the dozen later ones. This is different. Nobody knows what it might do when it comes."

They waited on the porch in the smell of roses and cut grass. "What time is it now?"

"One minute to five."

The needles flashed silver fire. They swam like a tiny school of metal fish in the darkening summer air.

Far away a mosquito sound. Then something like a tremor of drums. The three women cocked their heads, listening.

"We won't hear anything, will we?"

"They say not."

"Perhaps we're foolish. Perhaps we'll go right on, after five o'clock, shelling peas, opening doors, stirring soups, washing dishes, making lunches, peeling oranges . . ."

"My, how we'll laugh to think we were frightened by an old experiment!" They smiled a moment at each other.

"It's five o'clock."

At these words, hushed, they all busied themselves. Their fingers darted. Their faces were turned down to the motions they made. They made frantic patterns. They made lilacs

75

and grass and trees and houses and rivers in the embroidered cloth. They said nothing, but you could hear their breath in the silent porch air.

Thirty seconds passed.

The second woman sighed finally and began to relax.

"I think I just *will* go shell those peas for supper," she said. "I——"

But she hadn't time even to lift her head. Somewhere, at the side of her vision, she saw the world brighten and catch fire. She kept her head down, for she knew what it was. She didn't look up, nor did the others, and in the last instant their fingers were flying; they didn't glance about to see what was happening to the country, the town, this house, or even this porch. They were only staring down at the design in their flickering hands.

The second woman watched an embroidered flower go. She tried to embroider it back in, but it went, and then the road vanished, and the blades of grass. She watched a fire, in slow motion almost, catch upon the embroidered house and unshingle it, and pull each threaded leaf from the small green tree in the hoop, and she saw the sun itself pulled apart in the design. Then the fire caught upon the moving point of the needle while still it flashed; she watched the fire come along her fingers and arms and body, untwisting the yarn of her being so painstakingly that she could see it in all its devilish beauty, yanking out the pattern from the material at hand. What it was doing to the other women or the furniture or the elm tree in the yard, she never knew. For now, yes, now! it was plucking at the white embroidery of her flesh, the pink thread of her cheeks, and at last it found her heart, a soft red rose sewn with fire, and it burned the fresh, embroidered petals away, one by delicate one. . . .

12

THE BIG BLACK AND WHITE GAME

THE PEOPLE filled the stands behind the wire screen, waiting. Us kids, dripping from the lake, ran between the white cottages, past the resort hotel, screaming, and sat on the bleachers, making wet bottom marks. The hot sun beat down through the tall oak trees around the baseball diamond. Our fathers and mothers, in golf pants and light summer dresses, scolded us and made us sit still.

We looked toward the hotel and the back door of the vast kitchen, expectantly. A few colored women began walking across the shade-freckled area between, and in ten minutes the far left section of the bleachers was mellow with the color of their fresh-washed faces and arms. After all these years, whenever I think back on it, I can still hear the sounds they made. The sound on the warm air was like a soft moving of dove voices each time they talked among themselves.

Everybody quickened into amusement, laughter rose right up into the clear blue Wisconsin sky, as the kitchen door flung wide and out ran the big and little, the dark and high-yellar uniformed Negro waiters, janitors, bus boys, boatmen, cooks, bottle washers, soda jerks, gardeners, and golf-links tenders. They came capering, showing their fine white teeth, proud of their new red-striped uniforms, their shiny shoes rising and coming down on the green grass as they skirted the bleachers and drifted with lazy speed out on the field, calling to everybody and everything.

Us kids squealed. There was Long Johnson, the lawn-cutting man, and Cavanaugh, the soda-fountain man, and Shorty Smith and Pete Brown and Jiff Miller!

And *there* was Big Poe! Us kids shouted, applauded!

Big Poe was the one who stood so tall by the popcorn machine every night in the million-dollar dance pavilion farther down beyond the hotel on the lake rim. Every night I bought popcorn from Big Poe and he poured lots of butter all over it for me.

I stomped and yelled, "Big Poe! Big Poe!"

And he looked over at me and stretched his lips to bring out his teeth, waved, and shouted a laugh.

And Mama looked to the right, to the left, and back of us with worried eyes and nudged my elbow. "Hush," she said. "Hush."

"Land, land," said the lady next to my mother, fanning herself with a folded paper. "This is quite a day for the colored servants, ain't it? Only time of year they break loose. They look forward all summer to the big Black and White game. But this ain't nothing. You seen their Cakewalk Jamboree?"

"We got tickets for it," said Mother. "For tonight at the pavilion. Cost us a dollar each. That's pretty expensive, I'd say."

"But I always figure," said the woman, "once a year you got to spend. And it's really something to watch them dance. They just naturally got . . ."

"Rhythm," said Mother.

"That's the word," said the lady. "Rhythm. That's what they got. Land, you should see the colored maids up at the hotel. They been buying satin yardage in at the big store in Madison for a month now. And every spare minute they sit sewing and laughing. And I seen some of the feathers they bought for their hats. Mustard and wine ones and blue ones and violet ones. Oh, it'll be a sight!"

"They been airing out their tuxedos," I said. "I saw them hanging on lines behind the hotel all last week!"

"Look at them prance," said Mother. "You'd think they thought they were going to win the game from our men."

The colored men ran back and forth and yelled with their high, fluting voices and their low, lazy, interminable voices.

Way out in center field you could see the flash of teeth, their upraised naked black arms swinging and beating their sides as they hopped up and down and ran like rabbits, exuberantly.

Big Poe took a double fistful of bats, bundled them on his huge bull shoulder, and strutted along the first-base line, head back, mouth smiling wide open, his tongue moving, singing:

> "—gonna dance out both of my shoes,
> When they play those Jelly Roll Blues;
> Tomorrow night at the Dark Town Strutters' Ball!"

Up went his knees and down and out, swinging the bats like musical batons. A burst of applause and soft laughter came from the left-hand grandstands, where all the young, ripply colored girls with shiny brown eyes sat eager and easy. They made quick motions that were graceful and mellow because, maybe, of their rich coloring. Their laughter was like shy birds; they waved at Big Poe, and one of them with a high voice cried, "Oh, Big Poe! Oh, Big Poe!"

The white section joined politely in the applause as Big Poe finished his cakewalk. "Hey, Poe!" I yelled again.

"Stop that, Douglas!" said Mother, straight at me.

Now the white men came running between the trees with their uniforms on. There was a great thunder and shouting and rising up in our grandstand. The white men ran across the green diamond, flashing white.

"Oh, there's Uncle George!" said Mother. "My, doesn't he look nice?" And there was my uncle George toddling along in his outfit which didn't quite fit because Uncle has a potbelly, and jowls that sit out over any collar he puts on. He was hurrying along, trying to breathe and smile at the same time, lifting up his pudgy little legs. "My, they look so nice," enthused Mother.

I sat there, watching their movements. Mother sat beside me, and I think she was comparing and thinking, too, and what she saw amazed and disconcerted her. How easily the dark people had come running first, like those slow-motion deer and buck antelopes in those African moving pictures, like things in dreams. They came like beautiful brown, shiny animals that didn't know they were alive, but lived. And when they ran and put their easy, lazy, timeless legs out and followed them with their big, sprawling arms and loose fingers and smiled in the blowing wind, their expressions didn't say, "Look at me run, look at me run!" No, not at all. Their faces dreamily said, "Lord, but it's sure nice to run. See the ground swell soft under me? Gosh, I feel good. My muscles are

79

moving like oil on my bones and it's the best pleasure in the world to run." And they ran. There was no purpose to their running but exhilaration and living.

The white men worked at their running as they worked at everything. You felt embarrassed for them because they were alive too much in the wrong way. Always looking from the corners of their eyes to see if you were watching. The Negroes didn't care if you watched or not; they went on living, moving. They were so sure of playing that they didn't have to think about it any more.

"My, but our men look so nice," said my mother, repeating herself rather flatly. She had seen, compared the teams. Inside, she realized how laxly the colored men hung swaying in their uniforms, and how tensely, nervously, the white men were crammed, shoved, and belted into *their* outfits.

I guess the tenseness began then.

I guess everybody saw what was happening. They saw how the white men looked like senators in sun suits. And they admired the graceful unawareness of the colored men. And, as is always the case, that admiration turned to envy, to jealousy, to irritation. It turned to conversation like:

"That's my husband, Tom, on third base. Why doesn't he pick up his feet? He just *stands* there."

"Never you mind, never you mind. He'll pick 'em up when the time comes!"

"That's what *I* say! Now, take my Henry, for instance. Henry mightn't be active all the time, but when there's a crisis—just you *watch* him. Uh—I do wish he'd wave or something, though. Oh, *there!* Hello, Henry!"

"Look at that Jimmie Cosner playing around out there!"

I looked. A medium-sized white man with a freckled face and red hair was clowning on the diamond. He was balancing a bat on his forehead. There was laughter from the white grandstand. But it sounded like the kind of laughter you laugh when you're embarrassed for someone.

"Play ball!" said the umpire.

A coin was flipped. The colored men batted first.

"Darn it," said my mother.

The colored men ran in from the field happily.

Big Poe was first to bat. I cheered. He picked up the bat in one hand like a toothpick and idled over to the plate and laid the bat on his thick shoulder, smiling along its polished surface toward the stands where the colored women sat with their fresh flowery cream dresses stirring over their legs, which hung down between the seat intervals like crisp new sticks of ginger; their hair was all fancily spun and hung over their ears. Big Poe looked in particular at the little, dainty-as-a-chicken-bone shape of his girl friend Katherine.

She was the one who made the beds at the hotel and cottages every morning, who tapped on your door like a bird and politely asked if you was done dreaming, 'cause if you was she'd clean away all them old nightmares and bring in a fresh batch—please use them *one* at a time, thank yoah. Big Poe shook his head, looking at her, as if he couldn't believe she was there. Then he turned, one hand balancing the bat, his left hand dangling free at his side, to await the trial pitches. They hissed past, spatted into the open mouth of the catcher's mitt, were hurled back. The umpire grunted. The next pitch was the starter.

Big Poe let the first ball go by him.

"Stee-rike!" announced the umpire. Big Poe winked good-naturedly at the white folks. Bang! "Stee-rike two!" cried the umpire.

The ball came for the third time.

Big Poe was suddenly a greased machine pivoting; the dangling hand swept up to the butt end of the bat, the bat swiveled, connected with the ball—— *Whack!* The ball shot up into the sky, away down toward the wavering line of oak trees, down toward the lake, where a white sailboat slid silently by. The crowd yelled, me loudest! There went Uncle George, running on his stubby, wool-stockinged legs, getting smaller with distance.

Big Poe stood for a moment watching the ball go. Then he began to run. He went around the bases, loping, and on the way home from third base he waved to the colored girls naturally and happily and they waved back, standing on their seats and shrilling.

Ten minutes later, with the bases loaded and run after run being driven in, and Big Poe coming to bat again, my mother turned to me. "They're the most inconsiderate people," she said.

"But that's the game," I said. "They've only got two outs."

"But the score's seven to nothing," my mother protested.

"Well, just you wait until *our* men come to bat," said the lady next to my mother, waving away a fly with a pale blue-veined hand. "Those Negroes are too big for their britches."

"Stee-rike two!" said the umpire as Big Poe swung.

"All the past week at the hotel," said the woman next to my mother, staring out at Big Poe steadily, "the hotel service has been simply terrible. Those maids don't talk about a thing save the Cakewalk Jamboree, and whenever you want ice water it takes half an hour to fetch it, they're so busy sewing."

"Ball one!" said the umpire.

The woman fussed. "I'll be glad when this week's over, that's what I got to say," she said.

81

"Ball two!" said the umpire to Big Poe.

"Are they going to *walk* him?" asked my mother of me. "Are they *crazy*?" To the woman next to her: "That's right. They been acting funny all week. Last night I had to tell Big Poe twice to put extra butter on my popcorn. I guess he was trying to save money or something."

"Ball three!" said the umpire.

The lady next to my mother cried out suddenly and fanned herself furiously with her newspaper. "Land, I just *thought*. Wouldn't it be awful if they *won* the game? They *might*, you know. They might do it."

My mother looked at the lake, at the trees, at her hands. "I don't know why Uncle George had to play. Make a fool of himself. Douglas, you run tell him to quit right now. It's bad on his heart."

"You're out!" cried the umpire to Big Poe.

"Ah," sighed the grandstand.

The side was retired. Big Poe laid down his bat gently and walked along the base line. The white men pattered in from the field looking red and irritable, with big islands of sweat under their armpits. Big Poe looked over at me. I winked at him. He winked back. Then I knew he wasn't so dumb.

He'd struck out on purpose.

Long Johnson was going to pitch for the colored team.

He ambled out to the rubber, worked his fingers around in his fists to limber them up.

First white man to bat was a man named Kodimer, who sold suits in Chicago all year round.

Long Johnson fed them over the plate with tired, unassuming, controlled accuracy.

Mr. Kodimer chopped. Mr. Kodimer swatted. Finally Mr. Kodimer bunted the ball down the third-base line.

"Out at first base," said the umpire, an Irishman named Mahoney.

Second man up was a young Swede named Moberg. He hit a high fly to center field which was taken by a little plump Negro who didn't look fat because he moved around like a smooth, round glob of mercury.

Third man up was a Milwaukee truck driver. He whammed a line drive to center field. It was good. Except that he tried to stretch it into a two-bagger. When he pulled up at second base, there was Emancipated Smith with a white pellet in his dark, dark hand, waiting.

My mother sank back in her seat, exhaling. "Well, I *never*!"

"It's getting hotter," said the lady elbow-next. "Think I'll go for a stroll by the lake soon. It's too hot to sit and watch a silly game today. Mightn't you come along with me, missus?" she asked Mother.

It went on that way for five innings.

It was eleven to nothing and Big Poe had struck out three times on purpose, and in the last half of the fifth was when Jimmie Cosner came to bat for our side again. He'd been trying all afternoon, clowning, giving directions, telling everybody just where he was going to blast that pill once he got hold of it. He swaggered up toward the plate now, confident and bugle-voiced. He swung six bats in his thin hands, eying them critically with his shiny green little eyes. He chose one, dropped the others, ran to the plate, chopping out little islands of green fresh lawn with his cleated heels. He pushed his cap back on his dusty red hair. "Watch this!" he called out loud to the ladies. "You watch me show these dark boys! Ya-hah!"

Long Johnson on the mound did a slow serpentine windup. It was like a snake on a limb of a tree, uncoiling, suddenly darting at you. Instantly Johnson's hand was in front of him, open, like black fangs, empty. And the white pill slashed across the plate with a sound like a razor.

"Stee-rike!"

Jimmie Cosner put his bat down and stood glaring at the umpire. He said nothing for a long time. Then he spat deliberately near the catcher's foot, took up the yellow maple bat again, and swung it so the sun glinted the rim of it in a nervous halo. He twitched and sidled it on his thin-boned shoulder, and his mouth opened and shut over his long nicotined teeth.

Clap! went the catcher's mitt.

Cosner turned, stared.

The catcher, like a black magician, his white teeth gleaming, opened up his oily glove. There, like a white flower growing, was the baseball.

"Stee-rike two!" said the umpire, far away in the heat.

Jimmie Cosner laid his bat across the plate and hunched his freckled bands on his hips. "You mean to tell me that was a strike?"

"That's what I said," said the umpire. "Pick up the bat."

"To hit you on the head with," said Cosner sharply.

"Play ball or hit the showers!"

Jimmie Cosner worked his mouth to collect enough saliva to spit, then angrily swallowed it, swore a bitter oath instead. Reaching down, he raised the bat, poised it like a musket on his shoulder.

And here came the ball! It started out small and wound up big in front of him. Powie! An explosion off the yellow bat. The ball spiraled up and up. Jimmie lit out for first base. The ball paused, as if thinking about gravity up there in the sky. A wave came in on the shore of the lake and fell down. The crowd yelled. Jimmie ran. The ball made its decision, came down. A lithe high-yellar was under it, fumbled it. The ball spilled to the turf, was plucked up, hurled to first base.

Jimmie saw he was going to be out. So he jumped feet-first at the base.

Everyone saw his cleats go into Big Poe's ankle. Everybody saw the red blood. Everybody heard the shout, the shriek, saw the heavy clouds of dust rising.

"I'm safe!" protested Jimmie two minutes later.

Big Poe sat on the ground. The entire dark team stood around him. The doctor bent down, probed Big Poe's ankle, saying, "Mmmm," and "Pretty bad. Here." And he swabbed medicine on it and put a white bandage on it.

The umpire gave Cosner the cold-water eye. "Hit the showers!"

"Like hell!" said Cosner. And he stood on that first base, blowing his cheeks out and in, his freckled hands swaying at his sides. "I'm safe. I'm stayin' right here, by God! No nigger put *me* out!"

"No," said the umpire. "A white man did. *Me. Get!*"

"He dropped the ball! Look up the rules! I'm safe!"

The umpire and Cosner stood glaring at each other.

Big Poe looked up from having his swollen ankle tended. His voice was thick and gentle and his eyes examined Jimmie Cosner gently.

"Yes, he's safe, Mr. Umpire. Leave him stay. He's safe."

I was standing right there. I heard the whole thing. Me and some other kids had run out on the field to see. My mother kept calling me to come back to the stands.

"Yes, he's safe," said Big Poe again.

All the colored men let out a yell.

"What'sa matter with you, black boy? You get hit in the head?"

"You heard me," replied Big Poe quietly. He looked at the doctor bandaging him. "He's safe. Leave him stay."

The umpire swore.

"Okay, okay. So he's safe!"

The umpire stalked off, his back stiff, his neck red.

Big Poe was helped up. "Better not walk on that," cautioned the doctor.

"I can walk," whispered Big Poe carefully.

"Better not play."

"I can play," said Big Poe gently, certainly, shaking his head, wet streaks drying under his white eyes. "I'll play *good.*" He looked no place at all. "I'll play plenty good."

"Oh," said the second-base colored man. It was a funny sound.

All the colored men looked at each other, at Big Poe, then at Jimmie Cosner, at the sky, at the lake, the crowd. They walked off quietly to take their places. Big Poe stood with his bad foot hardly touching the ground, balanced. The doctor argued. But Big Poe waved him away.

"Batter up!" cried the umpire.

We got settled in the stands again. My mother pinched my leg and asked me why I couldn't sit still. It got warmer. Three or four more waves fell on the shore line. Behind the wire screen the ladies fanned their wet faces and the men inched their rumps forward on the wooden planks, held papers over their scowling brows to see Big Poe standing like a redwood tree out there on first base, Jimmie Cosner standing in the immense shade of that dark tree.

Young Moberg came up to bat for our side.

"Come on, Swede, come on, Swede!" was the cry, a lonely cry, like a dry bird, from out on the blazing green turf. It was Jimmie Cosner calling. The grandstand stared at him. The dark heads turned on their moist pivots in the outfield; the black faces came in his direction, looking him over, seeing his thin, nervously arched back. He was the center of the universe.

"Come on, Swede! Let's show these black boys!" laughed Cosner.

He trailed off. There was a complete silence. Only the wind came through the high, glittering trees.

"Come on, Swede, hang one on that old pill. . . ."

Long Johnson, on the pitcher's mound, cocked his head. Slowly, deliberately, he eyed Cosner. A look passed between him and Big Poe, and Jimmie Cosner saw the look and shut up and swallowed, hard.

Long Johnson took his time with his windup.

Cosner took a lead off base.

Long Johnson stopped loading his pitch.

Cosner skipped back to the bag, kissed his hand, and patted the kiss dead center on the bag. Then he looked up and smiled around.

Again the pitcher coiled up his long, hinged arm, curled loving dark fingers on the leather pellet, drew it back and— Cosner danced off first base. Cosner jumped up and down like a monkey. The pitcher did not look at him. The pitcher's eyes watched secretively, slyly, amusedly, sidewise. Then, snapping his head, the pitcher scared Cosner back to the bag. Cosner stood and jeered.

The third time Long Johnson made as if to pitch, Cosner was far off the bag and running toward second.

Snap went the pitcher's hand. *Boom* went the ball in Big Poe's glove at first base.

Everything was sort of frozen. Just for a second.

There was the sun in the sky, the lake and the boats on it, the grandstands, the pitcher on his mound standing with his hand out and down after tossing the ball; there was Big Poe with the ball in his mighty black hand; there was the infield staring, crouching in at the scene, and there was Jimmie Cosner running, kicking up dirt, the only moving thing in the entire summer world.

Big Poe leaned forward, sighted toward second base, drew back his mighty right hand, and hurled that white baseball straight down along the line until it reached Jimmie Cosner's head.

Next instant, the spell was broken.

Jimmie Cosner lay flat on the burning grass. People boiled out of the grandstands. There was swearing, and women screaming, a clattering of wood as the men rushed down the wooden boards of the bleachers. The colored team ran in from the field. Jimmie Cosner lay there. Big Poe, no expression on his face, limped off the field, pushing white men away from him like clothespins when they tried stopping him. He just picked them up and threw them away.

"Come on, Douglas!" shrieked Mother, grabbing me. "Let's get home! They might have razors! Oh!"

That night, after the near riot of the afternoon, my folks stayed home reading magazines. All the cottages around us were lighted. Everybody was home. Distantly I heard music. I slipped out the back door into the ripe summer-night darkness and ran toward the dance pavilion. All the lights were on, and music played.

But there were no white people at the tables. Nobody had come to the Jamboree.

There were only colored folks. Women in bright red and blue satin gowns and net stockings and soft gloves, with wine-plume hats, and men in glossy tuxedos. The music crashed out, up, down, and around the floor. And laughing and stepping high, flinging their polished shoes out and up in the cakewalk, were Long Johnson and Cavanaugh and Jiff Miller and Pete Brown, and—limping—Big Poe and Katherine, his girl, and all the other lawn-cutters and boatmen and janitors and chambermaids, all on the floor at one time.

It was so dark all around the pavilion; the stars shone in the black sky, and I stood outside, my nose against the window, looking in for a long, long time, silently.

I went to bed without telling anyone what I'd seen.

I just lay in the dark smelling the ripe apples in the dimness and hearing the lake at night and listening to that distant, faint and wonderful music. Just before I slept I heard those last strains again:

> "—gonna dance out both of my shoes,
> When they play those Jelly Roll Blues;
> Tomorrow night at the Dark Town Strutters' Ball!"

13

A SOUND OF THUNDER

THE SIGN on the wall seemed to quaver under a film of sliding warm water. Eckels felt his eyelids blink over his stare, and the sign burned in this momentary darkness:

> TIME SAFARI, INC.
> SAFARIS TO ANY YEAR IN THE PAST.
> YOU NAME THE ANIMAL.
> WE TAKE YOU THERE.
> YOU SHOOT IT.

A warm phlegm gathered in Eckels' throat; he swallowed and pushed it down. The muscles around his mouth formed a smile as he put his hand slowly out upon the air, and in that hand waved a check for ten thousand dollars to the man behind the desk.

"Does this safari guarantee I come back alive?"

"We guarantee nothing," said the official, "except the

dinosaurs." He turned. "This is Mr. Travis, your Safari Guide in the Past. He'll tell you what and where to shoot. If he says no shooting, no shooting. If you disobey instructions, there's a stiff penalty of another ten thousand dollars, plus possible government action, on your return."

Eckels glanced across the vast office at a mass and tangle, a snaking and humming of wires and steel boxes, at an aurora that flickered now orange, now silver, now blue. There was a sound like a gigantic bonfire burning all of Time, all the years and all the parchment calendars, all the hours piled high and set aflame.

A touch of the hand and this burning would, on the instant, beautifully reverse itself. Eckels remembered the wording in the advertisements to the letter. Out of chars and ashes, out of dust and coals, like golden salamanders, the old years, the green years, might leap; roses sweeten the air, white hair turn Irish-black, wrinkles vanish; all, everything fly back to seed, flee death, rush down to their beginnings, suns rise in western skies and set in glorious easts, moons eat themselves opposite to the custom, all and everything cupping one in another like Chinese boxes, rabbits in hats, all and everything returning to the fresh death, the seed death, the green death, to the time before the beginning. A touch of a hand might do it, the merest touch of a hand.

"Hell and damn," Eckels breathed, the light of the Machine on his thin face. "A real Time Machine." He shook his head. "Makes you think. If the election had gone badly yesterday, I might be here now running away from the results. Thank God Keith won. He'll make a fine President of the United States."

"Yes," said the man behind the desk. "We're lucky. If Deutscher had gotten in, we'd have the worst kind of dictatorship. There's an anti-everything man for you, a militarist, anti-Christ, anti-human, anti-intellectual. People called us up, you know, joking but not joking. Said if Deutscher became President they wanted to go live in 1492. Of course it's not our business to conduct Escapes, but to form Safaris. Anyway, Keith's President now. All you got to worry about is——"

"Shooting my dinosaur," Eckels finished it for him.

"*A Tyrannosaurus rex*. The Thunder Lizard, the damnedest monster in history. Sign this release. Anything happens to you, we're not responsible. Those dinosaurs are hungry."

Eckels flushed angrily. "Trying to scare me!"

"Frankly, yes. We don't want anyone going who'll panic at the first shot. Six Safari leaders were killed last year, and a dozen hunters. We're here to give you the damnedest thrill a *real* hunter ever asked for. Traveling you back sixty million years to bag the biggest damned game in all Time. Your personal check's still there. Tear it up."

Mr. Eckels looked at the check for a long time. His fingers twitched.

"Good luck," said the man behind the desk. "Mr. Travis, he's all yours."

They moved silently across the room, taking their guns with them, toward the Machine, toward the silver metal and the roaring light.

First a day and then a night and then a day and then a night, then it was day-night-day-night-day. A week, a month, a year, a decade! A.D. 2055. A.D. 2019. 1999! 1957! Gone! The Machine roared.

They put on their oxygen helmets and tested the intercoms.

Eckels swayed on the padded seat, his face pale, his jaw stiff. He felt the trembling in his arms and he looked down and found his hands tight on the new rifle. There were four other men in the Machine. Travis, the Safari Leader, his assistant, Lesperance, and two other hunters, Billings and Kramer. They sat looking at each other, and the years blazed around them.

"Can these guns get a dinosaur cold?" Eckels felt his mouth saying.

"If you hit them right," said Travis on the helmet radio. "Some dinosaurs have two brains, one in the head, another far down the spinal column. We stay away from those. That's stretching luck. Put your first two shots into the eyes, if you can, blind them, and go back into the brain."

The Machine howled. Time was a film run backward. Suns fled and ten million moons fled after them. "Good God," said Eckels. "Every hunter that ever lived would envy us today. This makes Africa seem like Illinois."

The Machine slowed; its scream fell to a murmur. The Machine stopped.

The sun stopped in the sky.

The fog that had enveloped the Machine blew away and they were in an old time, a very old time indeed, three hunters and two Safari Heads with their blue metal guns across their knees.

"Christ isn't born yet," said Travis. "Moses has not gone to the mountain to talk with God. The Pyramids are still in the earth, waiting to be cut out and put up. *Remember* that, Alexander, Caesar, Napoleon, Hitler—none of them exists."

The men nodded.

"That"—Mr. Travis pointed—"is the jungle of sixty million two thousand and fifty-five years before President Keith."

He indicated a metal path that struck off into green wilderness, over steaming swamp, among giant ferns and palms.

"And that," he said, "is the Path, laid by Time Safari for your use. It floats six inches above the earth. Doesn't touch so much as one grass blade, flower, or tree. It's an antigravity metal. Its purpose is to keep you from touching this world of the past in any way. Stay on the Path. Don't go off it. I repeat. *Don't go off.* For *any* reason! If you fall off, there's a penalty. And don't shoot any animal we don't okay."

"Why?" asked Eckels.

They sat in the ancient wilderness. Far birds' cries blew on a wind, and the smell of tar and an old salt sea, moist grasses, and flowers the color of blood.

"We don't want to change the Future. We don't belong here in the Past. The government doesn't *like* us here. We have to pay big graft to keep our franchise. A Time Machine is damn finicky business. Not knowing it, we might kill an important animal, a small bird, a roach, a flower even, thus destroying an important link in a growing species."

"That's not clear," said Eckels.

"All right," Travis continued, "say we accidentally kill one mouse here. That means all the future families of this one particular mouse are destroyed, right?"

"Right."

"And all the families of the families of that one mouse! With a stamp of your foot, you annihilate first one, then a dozen, then a thousand, a million, a *billion* possible mice!"

"So they're dead," said Eckels. "So what?"

"So what?" Travis snorted quietly. "Well, what about the foxes that'll need those mice to survive? For want of ten mice, a fox dies. For want of ten foxes, a lion starves. For want of a lion, all manner of insects, vultures, infinite billions of life forms are thrown into chaos and destruction. Eventually it all boils down to this: fifty-nine million years later, a cave man, one of a dozen on the *entire* world, goes hunting wild boar or saber-tooth tiger for food. But you, friend, have *stepped* on all the tigers in that region. By stepping on *one* single mouse. So the cave man starves. And the cave man, please note, is not just *any* expendable man, no! He is an *entire future nation.* From his loins would have sprung ten sons. From *their* loins one hundred sons, and thus onward to a civilization. Destroy this one man, and you destroy a race, a people, an entire history of life. It is comparable to slaying some of Adam's grandchildren. The stomp of your foot, on one mouse, could start an earthquake, the effects of which could shake our earth and destinies down through Time, to their very foundations. With the death of that one cave man, a billion others yet unborn are throttled in the womb. Perhaps Rome never rises on its seven hills. Perhaps Europe is forever a dark forest, and only Asia waxes healthy and teeming. Step on a mouse and you crush the Pyramids. Step on a mouse and you leave your print, like a Grand Canyon, across Eternity. Queen Elizabeth might never be born, Washington might not cross the Delaware, there might never be a United States at all. So be careful. Stay on the Path. *Never* step off!"

"I see," said Eckels. "Then it wouldn't pay for us even to touch the *grass?*"

"Correct. Crushing certain plants could add up infinitesimally. A little error here would multiply in sixty million years, all out of proportion. Of course maybe our theory is wrong. Maybe Time *can't* be changed by us. Or maybe it can be changed only in little subtle ways. A dead mouse here makes an insect imbalance there, a population disproportion later, a bad harvest further on, a depression, mass starvation, and, finally, a change in *social* temperament in far-flung countries. Something much more subtle, like that. Perhaps only a soft breath, a whisper, a hair, pollen on the air, such a slight, slight change that unless you looked close you wouldn't see it. Who knows? Who really can say he knows? We don't know. We're guessing. But until we do know for certain whether our messing around in Time *can* make a big roar or a little rustle in history, we're being damned careful. This Machine, this Path, your clothing and bodies, were sterilized, as you know, before the journey. We wear these oxygen helmets so we can't introduce our bacteria into an ancient atmosphere."

"How do we know which animals to shoot?"

"They're marked with red paint," said Travis. "Today, before our journey, we sent Lesperance here back with the Machine. He came to this particular era and followed certain animals."

"Studying them?"

"Right," said Lesperance. "I track them through their entire existence, noting which of them lives longest. Very few. How many times they mate. Not often. Life's short. When I find one that's going to die when a tree falls on him, or one that drowns in a tar pit, I note the exact hour, minute, and second. I shoot a paint bomb. It leaves a red patch on his hide. We can't miss it. Then I correlate our arrival in the Past so that we meet the Monster not more than two minutes before he would have died anyway. This way, we kill

92

only animals with no future, that are never going to mate again. You see how *careful* we are?"

"But if you came back this morning in Time," said Eckels eagerly, "you must've bumped into *us*, our Safari! How did it turn out? Was it successful? Did all of us get through—alive?"

Travis and Lesperance gave each other a look.

"That'd be a paradox," said the latter. "Time doesn't permit that sort of mess—a man meeting himself. When such occasions threaten, Time steps aside. Like an airplane hitting an air pocket. You felt the Machine jump just before we stopped? That was us passing ourselves on the way back to the Future. We saw nothing. There's no way of telling *if* this expedition was a success, *if* we got our monster, or whether all of—meaning *you*, Mr. Eckels—got out alive."

Eckels smiled palely.

"Cut that," said Travis sharply. "Everyone on his feet!"

They were ready to leave the Machine.

The jungle was high and the jungle was broad and the jungle was the entire world forever and forever. Sounds like music and sounds like flying tents filled the sky, and those were pterodactyls soaring with cavernous gray wings, gigantic bats out of a delirium and a night fever. Eckles, balanced on the narrow Path, aimed his rifle playfully.

"Stop that!" said Travis. "Don't even aim for fun, damn it! If your gun should go off——"

Eckels flushed. "Where's our *Tyrannosaurus?*"

Lesperance checked his wrist watch. "Up ahead. We'll bisect his trail in sixty seconds. Look for the red paint, for Christ's sake. Don't shoot till we give the word. Stay on the Path. *Stay on the Path!*"

They moved forward in the wind of morning.

"Strange," murmured Eckels. "Up ahead, sixty million years, Election Day over. Keith made President. Everyone celebrating. And here we are, a million years lost, and they don't exist. The things we worried about for months, a lifetime, not even born or thought about yet."

"Safety catches off, everyone!" ordered Travis. "You, first shot, Eckels. Second, Billings. Third, Kramer."

"I've hunted tiger, wild boar, buffalo, elephant, but Jesus, this is *it*," said Eckels. "I'm shaking like a kid."

"Ah," said Travis.

Everyone stopped.

Travis raised his hand. "Ahead," he whispered. "In the mist. There he is. There's His Royal Majesty now."

The jungle was wide and full of twitterings, rustlings, murmurs, and sighs.

Suddenly it all ceased, as if someone had shut a door. Silence.

A sound of thunder.

Out of the mist, one hundred yards away, came *Tyrannosaurus rex*.

"Jesus God," whispered Eckels.

"Sh!"

It came on great oiled, resilient, striding legs. It towered thirty feet above half of the trees, a great evil god, folding its delicate watchmaker's claws close to its oily reptilian chest. Each lower leg was a piston, a thousand pounds of white bone, sunk in thick ropes of muscle, sheathed over in a gleam of pebbled skin like the mail of a terrible warrior. Each thigh was a ton of meat, ivory, and steel mesh. And from the great breathing cage of the upper body those two delicate arms dangled out front, arms with hands which might pick up and examine men like toys, while the snake neck coiled. And the head itself, a ton of sculptured stone, lifted easily upon the sky. Its mouth gaped, exposing a fence of teeth like daggers. Its eyes rolled, ostrich eggs, empty of all expression save hunger. It closed its mouth in a death grin. It ran, its pelvic bones crushing aside trees and bushes, its taloned feet clawing damp earth, leaving prints six inches deep wherever it settled its weight. It ran with a gliding ballet step, far too poised and balanced for its ten tons. It moved into a sunlit arena warily, its beautifully reptile hands feeling the air.

"My God!" Eckels twitched his mouth. "It could reach up and grab the moon."

"Sh!" Travis jerked angrily. "He hasn't seen us yet."

"It can't be killed." Eckels pronounced this verdict quietly, as if there could be no argument. He had weighed the evidence and this was his considered opinion. The rifle in his hands seemed a cap gun. "We were fools to come. This is impossible."

"Shut up!" hissed Travis.

"Nightmare."

"Turn around," commanded Travis. "Walk quietly to the Machine. We'll remit one-half your fee."

"I didn't realize it would be this *big*," said Eckels. "I miscalculated, that's all. And now I want out."

"It sees us!"

"There's the red paint on its chest!"

The Thunder Lizard raised itself. Its armored flesh glittered like a thousand green coins. The coins, crusted with slime, steamed. In the slime, tiny insects wriggled, so that the entire body seemed to twitch and undulate, even while the monster itself did not move. It exhaled. The stink of raw flesh blew down the wilderness.

"Get me out of here," said Eckels. "It was never like this before. I was always sure I'd come through alive. I had good guides, good safaris, and safety. This time, I figured wrong. I've met my match and admit it. This is too much for me to get hold of."

"Don't run," said Lesperance. "Turn around. Hide in the Machine."

"Yes." Eckels seemed to be numb. He looked at his feet as if trying to make them move. He gave a grunt of helplessness.

"Eckels!"

He took a few steps, blinking, shuffling.

"Not *that* way!"

The Monster, at the first motion, lunged forward with a terrible scream. It covered one hundred yards in four seconds. The rifles jerked up and blazed fire. A windstorm from the beast's mouth engulfed them in the stench of slime and old blood. The Monster roared, teeth glittering with sun.

Eckels, not looking back, walked blindly to the edge of the Path, his gun limp in his arms, stepped off the Path, and walked, not knowing it, in the jungle. His feet sank into green moss. His legs moved him, and he felt alone and remote from the events behind.

The rifles cracked again. Their sound was lost in shriek and lizard thunder. The great lever of the reptile's tail swung up, lashed sideways. Trees exploded in clouds of leaf and branch. The Monster twitched its jeweler's hands down to fondle at the men, to twist them in half, to crush them like berries, to cram them into its teeth and its screaming throat. Its boulder-stone eyes leveled with the men. They saw themselves mirrored. They fired at the metallic eyelids and the blazing black iris.

Like a stone idol, like a mountain avalanche, *Tyrannosaurus* fell. Thundering, it clutched trees, pulled them with it. It wrenched and tore the metal Path. The men flung themselves back and away. The body hit, ten tons of cold flesh and stone. The guns fired. The Monster lashed its armored tail, twitched its snake jaws, and lay still. A fount of blood spurted from its throat. Somewhere inside, a sac of fluids burst. Sickening gushes drenched the hunters. They stood, red and glistening.

The thunder faded.

The jungle was silent. After the avalanche, a green peace. After the nightmare, morning.

Billings and Kramer sat on the pathway and threw up. Travis and Lesperance stood with smoking rifles, cursing steadily.

In the Time Machine, on his face, Eckels lay shivering.

95

He had found his way back to the Path, climbed into the Machine.

Travis came walking, glanced at Eckels, took cotton gauze from a metal box, and returned to the others, who were sitting on the Path.

"Clean up."

They wiped the blood from their helmets. They began to curse too. The Monster lay, a hill of solid flesh. Within, you could hear the sighs and murmurs as the furthest chambers of it died, the organs malfunctioning, liquids running a final instant from pocket to sac to spleen, everything shutting off, closing up forever. It was like standing by a wrecked locomotive or a steam shovel at quitting time, all valves being released or levered tight. Bones cracked; the tonnage of its own flesh, off balance, dead weight, snapped the delicate forearms, caught underneath. The meat settled, quivering.

Another cracking sound. Overhead, a gigantic tree branch broke from its heavy mooring, fell. It crashed upon the dead beast with finality.

"There." Lesperance checked his watch. "Right on time. That's the giant tree that was scheduled to fall and kill this animal originally." He glanced at the two hunters. "You want the trophy picture?"

"What?"

"We can't take a trophy back to the Future. The body has to stay right here where it would have died originally, so the insects, birds, and bacteria can get at it, as they were intended to. Everything in balance. The body stays. But we *can* take a picture of you standing near it."

The two men tried to think, but gave up, shaking their heads.

They let themselves be led along the metal Path. They sank wearily into the Machine cushions. They gazed back at the ruined Monster, the stagnating mound, where already strange reptilian birds and golden insects were busy at the steaming armor.

A sound on the floor of the Time Machine stiffened them. Eckels sat there, shivering.

"I'm sorry," he said at last.

"Get up!" cried Travis.

Eckels got up.

"Go out on that Path alone," said Travis. He had his rifle pointed. "You're not coming back in the Machine. We're leaving you here!"

Lesperance seized Travis' arm. "Wait——"

"Stay out of this!" Travis shook his hand away. "This son of a bitch nearly killed us. But it isn't *that* so much. Hell, no.

It's his *shoes!* Look at them! He ran off the Path. My God, that *ruins* us! Christ knows how much we'll forfeit. Tens of thousands of dollars of insurance! We guarantee no one leaves the Path. He left it. Oh, the damn fool! I'll have to report to the government. They might revoke our license to travel. God knows *what* he's done to Time, to History!"

"Take it easy, all he did was kick up some dirt."

"How do we *know?*" cried Travis. "We don't know anything! It's all a damn mystery! Get out there, Eckels!"

Eckels fumbled his shirt. "I'll pay anything. A hundred thousand dollars!"

Travis glared at Eckels' checkbook and spat. "Go out there. The Monster's next to the Path. Stick your arms up to your elbows in his mouth. Then you can come back with us."

"That's unreasonable!"

"The Monster's dead, you yellow bastard. The bullets! The bullets can't be left behind. They don't belong in the Past; they might change something. Here's my knife. Dig them out!"

The jungle was alive again, full of the old tremorings and bird cries. Eckels turned slowly to regard the primeval garbage dump, that hill of nightmares and terror. After a long time, like a sleepwalker, he shuffled out along the Path.

He returned, shuddering, five minutes later, his arms soaked and red to the elbows. He held out his hands. Each held a number of steel bullets. Then he fell. He lay where he fell, not moving.

"You didn't have to make him do that," said Lesperance.

"Didn't I? It's too early to tell." Travis nudged the still body. "He'll live. Next time he won't go hunting game like this. Okay." He jerked his thumb wearily at Lesperance. "Switch on. Let's go home."

1492.   1776.   1812.

They cleaned their hands and faces. They changed their caking shirts and pants. Eckels was up and around again, not speaking. Travis glared at him for a full ten minutes.

"Don't look at me," cried Eckels. "I haven't done anything."

"Who can tell?"

"Just ran off the Path, that's all, a little mud on my shoes —what do you want me to do—get down and pray?"

"We might need it. I'm warning you, Eckels, I might kill you yet. I've got my gun ready."

"I'm innocent. I've done nothing!"

1999.   2000.   2055.
The Machine stopped.

"Get out," said Travis.

The room was there as they had left it. But not the same as they had left it. The same man sat behind the same desk. But the same man did not quite sit behind the same desk.

Travis looked around swiftly. "Everything okay here?" he snapped.

"Fine. Welcome home!"

Travis did not relax. He seemed to be looking at the very atoms of the air itself, at the way the sun poured through the one high window.

"Okay, Eckels, get out. Don't ever come back."

Eckels could not move.

"You heard me," said Travis. "What're you *staring* at?"

Eckels stood smelling of the air, and there was a thing to the air, a chemical taint so subtle, so slight, that only a faint cry of his subliminal senses warned him it was there. The colors, white, gray, blue, orange, in the wall, in the furniture, in the sky beyond the window, were . . . were . . . And there was a *feel*. His flesh twitched. His hands twitched. He stood drinking the oddness with the pores of his body. Somewhere, someone must have been screaming one of those whistles that only a dog can hear. His body screamed silence in return. Beyond this room, beyond this wall, beyond this man who was not quite the same man seated at this desk that was not quite the same desk . . . lay an entire world of streets and people. What sort of world it was now, there was no telling. He could feel them moving there, beyond the walls, almost, like so many chess pieces blown in a dry wind. . . .

But the immediate thing was the sign painted on the office wall, the same sign he had read earlier today on first entering.

Somehow, the sign had changed:

> TYME SEFARI INC.
> SEFARIS TU ANY YEER EN THE PAST.
> YU NAIM THE ANIMALL.
> WEE TAEK YOU THAIR.
> YU SHOOT ITT.

Eckels felt himself fall into a chair. He fumbled crazily at the thick slime on his boots. He held up a clod of dirt, trembling. "No, it *can't* be. Not a *little* thing like that. No!"

Embedded in the mud, glistening green and gold and black, was a butterfly, very beautiful, and very dead.

"Not a little thing like *that!* Not a butterfly!" cried Eckels.

It fell to the floor, an exquisite thing, a small thing that could upset balances and knock down a line of small dominoes and then big dominoes and then gigantic dominoes, all down the years across Time. Eckels' mind whirled. It *couldn't* change things. Killing one butterfly couldn't be *that* important! Could it?

His face was cold. His mouth trembled, asking: "Who—who won the presidential election yesterday?"

The man behind the desk laughed. "You joking? You know damn well. Deutscher, of course! Who else? Not that damn weakling Keith. We got an iron man now, a man with guts, by God!" The official stopped. "What's wrong?"

Eckels moaned. He dropped to his knees. He scrabbled at the golden butterfly with shaking fingers. "Can't we," he pleaded to the world, to himself, to the officials, to the Machine, "can't we take it *back*, can't we *make* it alive again? Can't we start over? Can't we——"

He did not move. Eyes shut, he waited, shivering. He heard Travis breathe loud in the room; he heard Travis shift his rifle, click the safety catch, and raise the weapon.

There was a sound of thunder.

14

THE GREAT WIDE WORLD OVER THERE

It was a day to be out of bed, to pull curtains and fling open windows. It was a day to make your heart bigger with warm mountain air.

Cora, feeling like a young girl in a wrinkled old dress, sat up in bed.

It was early, the sun barely on the horizon, but already the birds were stirring from the pines and ten billion red ants milled free from their bronze hills by the cabin door. Cora's husband Tom slept like a bear in a snowy hibernation of bedclothes beside her. Will my heart wake him up? she wondered.

And then she knew why this seemed a special day.

"Benjy's coming!"

She imagined him far off, leaping green meadows, fording streams where spring was pushing itself in cool colors of moss and clear water toward the sea. She saw his great shoes dusting and flicking the stony roads and paths. She saw his freckled face high in the sun looking giddily down his long body at his distant hands flying out and back behind him.

Benjy, come on! she thought, opening a window swiftly.

Wind blew her hair like a gray spider web about her cold ears. Now Benjy's at Iron Bridge, now at Meadow Pike, now up Creek Path, over Chesley's Field . . .

Somewhere in those Missouri mountains was Benjy. Cora blinked. Those strange high hills beyond which twice a year she and Tom drove their horse and wagon to town, and through which, thirty years ago, she had wanted to run forever, saying, "Oh, Tom, let's just drive and drive until we reach the sea." But Tom had looked at her as if she had slapped his face, and he had turned the wagon around and driven on home, talking to the mare. And if people lived by shores where the sea came like a storm, now louder, now softer, every day, she did not know it. And if there were cities where neons were like pink ice and green mint and red fireworks each evening, she didn't know that either. Her horizon, north, south, east, west, was this valley, and had never been anything else.

But now, today, she thought, Benjy's coming from that world out there; he's seen it, smelt it; he'll tell me about it. And he can write. She looked at her hands. He'll be here a whole month and teach me. Then I can write out into that world and bring it here to the mailbox I'll make Tom build today. "Get up, Tom! You *hear?*"

She put her hand out to push the bank of sleeping snow.

By nine o'clock the valley was full of grasshoppers flinging themselves through the blue, piney air, while smoke curled into the sky.

Cora, singing into her pots and pans as she polished them, saw her wrinkled face bronzed and freshened in the copper bottoms. Tom was grumbling the sounds of a sleepy bear at his mush breakfast, while her singing moved all about him, like a bird in a cage.

"*Someone's* mighty happy," said a voice.

Cora made herself into a statue. From the corners of her eyes she saw a shadow cross the room.

"Mrs. Brabbam?" asked Cora of her scouring cloth.

"That's who it is!" And there stood the Widow Lady, her gingham dress dragging the warm dust, her letters in her chickeny hand. "Morning! I just been to my mailbox. Got me a real beauty of a letter from my uncle George in Springfield." Mrs. Brabbam fixed Cora with a gaze like a silver needle. "How long since you got a letter from your uncle, missus?"

"My uncles are all dead." It was not Cora herself, but her tongue, that lied. When the time came, she knew, it would be her tongue alone that must take communion and confess earthly sinning.

"It's certainly *nice*, getting mail." Mrs. Brabbam waved her letters in a straight flush on the morning air.

Always twisting the knife in the flesh. How many years, thought Cora, had this run on, Mrs. Brabbam and her smily eyes, talking loud of how she got mail; implying that nobody else for miles around could read? Cora bit her lip and almost threw the pot, but set it down, laughing. "I forgot to tell you. My nephew Benjy's coming; his folks are poorly, and he's here for the summer today. He'll teach me to write. And Tom's building us a postal box, aren't you, Tom?"

Mrs. Brabbam clutched her letters. "Well, isn't that fine! You *lucky* lady." And suddenly the door was empty. Mrs. Brabbam was gone.

But Cora was after her. For in that instant she had seen something like a scarecrow, something like a flicker of pure sunlight, something like a brook trout jumping upstream, leap a fence in the yard below. She saw a huge hand wave and birds flush in terror from a crab-apple tree.

Cora was rushing, the world rushing back of her, down the path. "Benjy!"

They ran at each other like partners in a Saturday dance, linked arms, collided, and waltzed, jabbering. "Benjy!"

She glanced swiftly behind his ear.

Yes, *there* was the yellow pencil.

"Benjy, welcome!"

"Why, ma'am!" He held her off at arm's length. "Why, ma'am, you're *crying*."

"Here's my nephew," said Cora.

Tom scowled up from spooning his corn-meal mush.

"Mighty glad," smiled Benjy.

Cora held his arm tight so he couldn't vanish. She felt faint, wanting to sit, stand, run, but she only beat her heart fast and laughed at strange times. Now, in an instant, the far countries were brought near; here was this tall boy, lighting up the room like a pine torch, this boy who had seen cities and seas and been places when things had been better for his parents.

"Benjy, I got peas, corn, bacon, mush, soup, and beans for breakfast."

"Hold on!" said Tom.

"Hush, Tom, the boy's down to the bone with walking." She turned to the boy. "Benjy, tell me all about yourself. You *did* go to school?"

Benjy kicked off his shoes. With one bare foot he traced a word in the hearth ashes.

Tom scowled. "What's it say?"

"It says," said Benjy, "C and O and R and A. *Cora*."

"*My* name, Tom, see it! Oh, Benjy, it's good you really write, child. We had one cousin here, long ago, claimed he could spell upside down and backwards. So we fattened him up and he wrote letters but we never got answers. Come to find out he knew just enough spelling to mail letters to the dead-letter office. Lord, Tom knocked two months' worth of vittles out of that boy, batting him up the road with a piece of fence."

They laughed anxiously.

"I write fine," said the serious boy.

"That's all we want to know." She shoved a cut of berry pie at him. "Eat."

By ten-thirty, with the sun riding higher, after watching Benjy devour heaped platters of food, Tom thundered from the cabin; jamming his cap on. "I'm going out, by God, and cut down half the forest!" he said angrily.

But no one heard. Cora was seated in a breathless spell. She was watching the pencil behind Benjy's peach-fuzz ear. She saw him finger it casually, lazily, indifferently. Oh, not so casual, Benjy, she thought. Handle it like a spring robin's egg. She wanted to touch the pencil, but hadn't touched one in years because it made her feel foolish and then angry and then sad. Her hand twitched in her lap.

"You got some paper?" asked Benjy.

"Oh, land, I never thought," she wailed, and the room walls darkened. "What'll we do?"

"Just happens I brought some." He fetched a tablet from his little bag. "You want to write a letter somewhere?"

She smiled outrageously. "I want to write a letter to . . . to . . ." Her face fell apart. She looked around for someone in the distance. She looked at the mountains in the morning sunshine. She heard the sea rolling off on yellow shores a thousand miles away. The birds were coming north over the valley, on their way to multitudes of cities indifferent to her need at this instant.

"Benjy, why, I never thought until this moment. I don't know anybody in all the world out there. Nobody but my aunt. And if I wrote her it'd make her feel bad, a hundred miles from here, to have to find someone else to read the letter to her. She's got a whale-boned-corset sort of pride. Make her nervous the next ten years, that letter setting in her house on the mantel. No, no letter to her." Cora's eyes moved from the hills and the unseen ocean. "Who then? Where? Someone. I just've got to get me some letters."

"Hold on." Benjy fished a dime magazine from his coat. It had a red cover of an undressed lady screaming away from a green monster. "All sorts of addresses in here."

They leafed the pages together. "What's this?" Cora tapped an ad.

" 'HERE'S YOUR *Power Plus* FREE MUSCLE CHART. Send name, address,' " read Benjy, " 'to Dept. M-3 for Free Health Map!' "

"And what about *this* one?"

" 'DETECTIVES MAKE SECRET INVESTIGATIONS, PARTICULARS FREE. WRITE G.D.M. DETECTIVE SCHOOL——' "

"Everything's free. Well, Benjy." She looked at the pencil in his hand. He drew up his chair. She watched him turn the pencil in his fingers, making minor adjustments. She saw him bite his tongue softly. She saw him squint his eyes. She held her breath. She bent forward. She squinted her own eyes and clamped her tongue.

Now, now Benjy raised his pencil, licked it, and set it down to the paper.

There it is, thought Cora.

The first words. They formed themselves slowly on the incredible paper.

Dear Power Plus Muscle Company
Sirs, [he wrote].

The morning blew away on a wind, the morning flowed down the creek, the morning flew off with some ravens, and the sun burned on the cabin roof. Cora didn't turn when she heard a shuffle at the blazing, sun-filled door. Tom was there, but not there; nothing was before her but a series of filled pages, a whispering pencil, and Benjy's Palmer Penmanship hand. Cora moved her head around, around, with each *o*, each *l*, with each small hill of an *m;* each tiny dot made her head peck like a chicken; each crossed *t* made her tongue lick across her upper lip.

"It's noon and I'm hungry!" said Tom almost behind her.

But Cora was a statue now, watching the pencil as one watches a snail leaving an exceptional trail across a flat stone in the early morning.

"It's noon!" cried Tom again.

Cora glanced up, stunned.

"Why, it seems only a moment ago we wrote to that Philadelphia Coin Collecting Company, ain't that right, Benjy?" Cora smiled a smile much too dazzling for a woman fifty-five years old. "While you wait for your vittles, Tom, just can't you build that mailbox? Bigger than Mrs. Brabbam's, please?"

"I'll nail up a shoe box."

"Tom Gibbs." She rose pleasantly. Her smile said, Better run, better work, better *do!* "I want a big, pretty mailbox.

All white, for Benjy to paint our name on in black spelling. I won't have an shoe box for my very first real letter."

And it was done.

Benjy lettered the finished mailbox: MRS. CORA GIBBS, while Tom stood grumbling behind him.

"What's it say?"

" 'MR. TOM GIBBS,' " said Benjy quietly, painting.

Tom blinked at it for a minute, quietly, and then said, "I'm *still* hungry. Someone light the fire."

There were no stamps. Cora turned white. Tom was made to hitch up the horse and drive to Green Fork to buy some red ones, a green, and ten pink stamps with dignified gentlemen printed on them. But Cora rode along to be certain Tom didn't hurl these first letters in the creek. When they rode home, the first thing Cora did, face glowing, was poke in the new mailbox.

"You crazy?" said Tom.

"No harm looking."

That afternoon she visited the mailbox six times. On the seventh, a woodchuck jumped out. Tom stood laughing in the door, pounding his knees. Cora chased him out of the house, still laughing.

Then she stood in the window looking down at her mailbox right across from Mrs. Brabbam's. Ten years ago the Widow Lady had plunked her letter box right under Cora's nose, almost, when she could as easily have built it up nearer her own cabin. But it gave Mrs. Brabbam an excuse to float like a flower on a river down the hill path, flip the box wide with a great coughing and rustling, from time to time spying to see if Cora was watching. Cora always was. When caught, she pretended to sprinkle flowers with an empty watering can, or pick mushrooms in the wrong season.

Next morning Cora was up before the sun had warmed the strawberry patch or the wind had stirred the pines.

Benjy was sitting up in his cot when Cora returned from the mailbox. "Too early," he said. "Postman won't drive by yet."

"*Drive* by?"

"They come in cars this far out."

"Oh." Cora sat down.

"You sick, Aunt Cora?"

"No, no." She blinked. "It's just, I don't recall in twenty years seeing no mail truck whistle by here. It just came to me. All this time, I never seen no mailman at all."

"Maybe he comes when you're not around."

"I'm up with the fog spunks, down with the chickens. I

never really gave it a thought, of course, but——" She turned to look out the window, up at Mrs. Brabbam's house. "Benjy, I got a kind of sneaking hunch." She stood up and walked straight out of the cabin, down the dust path, Benjy following, across the thin road to Mrs. Brabbam's mailbox. A hush was on the fields and hills. It was so early it made you whisper.

"Don't break the law, Aunt Cora!"

"Shh! Here." She opened the box, put her hand in like someone fumbling in a gopher hole. "And here, and here." She rattled some letters into his cupped hands.

"Why, these been opened already! You open these, Aunt Cora?"

"Child, I never touched them." Her face was stunned. "This is the first time in my life I ever even let my shadow touch this box."

Benjy turned the letters around and around, cocking his head. "Why, Aunt Cora, these letters, they're ten years old!"

"What!" Cora grabbed at them.

"Aunt Cora, that lady's been getting the same mail every day for years. And they're not even addressed to Mrs. Brabbam, they're to some woman named Ortega in Green Fork."

"Ortega, the Mexican grocery woman! All these years," whispered Cora, staring at the worn mail in her hands. "All these years."

They gazed up at Mrs. Brabbam's sleeping house in the cool quiet morning.

"Oh, that sly woman, making a commotion with her letters, making me feel small. All puffed out she was, swishing along, reading her mail."

Mrs. Brabbam's front door opened.

"Put them back, Aunt Cora!"

Cora slammed the mailbox shut with time to spare.

Mrs. Brabbam drifted down the path, stopping here or there, quietly, to peer at the opening wild flowers.

"Morning," she said sweetly.

"Mrs. Brabbam, this is my nephew Benjy."

"How nice." Mrs. Brabbam, with a great swivel of her body, a flourish of her flour-white hands, rapped the mailbox as if to shake the letters loose inside, flipped the lid, and extracted the mail, covering her actions with her back. She made motions, and spun about merrily, winking. "Wonderful! Why, just look at this letter from dear Uncle George!"

"Well, ain't that *nice!*" said Cora.

Then the breathless summer days of waiting. The butterflies jumping orange and blue on the air, the flowers nodding

106

about the cabin, and the hard, constant sound of Benjy's pencil scribbling through the afternoons. Benjy's mouth was always packed with food, and Tom was always stomping in, to find lunch or supper late, cold, or both, or none at all.

Benjy handled the pencil with a delicious spread of his bony hands, lovingly inscribing each vowel and consonant as Cora hovered about him, making up words, rolling them on her tongue, delighted each time she saw them roll out on the paper. But she wasn't learning to write. "It's so much fun watching you write, Benjy. Tomorrow I'll start learning. Now take another letter!"

They worked their way through ads about Asthma, Trusses and Magic, they joined the Rosicrucians, or at least sent for a free Sealed Book all about the Knowledge that had been damned to oblivion, Secrets from Hidden ancient temples and buried sanctuaries. Then there were free packets of Giant Sunflower seeds, and something about HEARTBURN. They had worked back to page 127 of *Quarter Murder Magazine* on a bright summer morning when . . .

"Listen!" said Cora.

They listened.

"A car," said Benjy.

And up the blue hills and through the tall fiery green pines and along the dusty road, mile by mile, came the sound of a car riding along and along, until finally, at the bend, it came full thundering, and in an instant Cora was out of the door running, and as she ran she heard and saw and felt many things. First, from the corner of her eye, she saw Mrs. Brabbam gliding down the road from the other direction. Mrs. Brabbam froze when she saw the bright green car boiling on the grade, and there was the whistle of a silver whistle and the old man in the car leaned out just before Cora arrived and said, "Mrs. Gibbs?" "Yes!" she cried. "Mail for you, ma'am," he said, and held it toward her. She put out her hand, then drew it back, remembering. "Oh," she said, "please, would you mind, would you put it, please . . . in my mailbox?" The old man squinted at her, at the mailbox, back at her, and laughed. "Don't mind," he said, and did just that, put the mail in the box.

Mrs. Brabbam stood where she was, not moving, eyes wild. "Any mail for Mrs. Brabbam?" asked Cora.

"That's all." And the car dusted away down the road.

Mrs. Brabbam stood with her hands clenched together. Then, without looking in her own letter box, turned and rustled swiftly up her path, out of sight.

Cora walked around her mailbox twice, not touching it for a long time. "Benjy, I've got me some letters!" She reached in delicately and took them out and turned them over. She put them quietly in his hand. "Read them to me. Is my name on the front?"

"Yes'm." He opened the first letter with due carefulness and read it aloud in the summer morning:

" 'Dear Mrs. Gibbs . . .' "

He stopped and let her savor it, her eyes half shut, her mouth moving the words. He repeated it for artistic emphasis and then went on: " 'We are sending you our free folder, enclosed, from the Intercontinental Mailing Schools concerning full particulars on how you, too, can take our Correspondence Course in Sanitary Engineering——' "

"Benjy, Benjy, I'm so happy! Start over again!"

" 'Dear Mrs. Gibbs,' " he read.

After that the mailbox was never empty. The world came rushing and crowding in, all the places she had never seen or heard about or been to. Travel folders, spicecake recipes, and even a letter from an elderly gentleman who wished for a lady "—fifty years old, gentle disposition, money; object matrimony." Benjy wrote back, "I am already married, but thank you for your kind and thoughtful consideration. Yours truly, Cora Gibbs."

And the letters continued to pour across the hills, coin collectors' catalogues, Dime Novelty books, Magic List Numbers, Arthritis Charts, Flea Killer Samples. The world filled up her letter box, and suddenly she was not alone or remote from people. If a man wrote a form letter to Cora about the Mysteries of Ancient Maya Revealed, he was likely as not to receive three letters from Cora in the next week, budding out their formal meeting into a warm friendship. After one particularly hard day of writing, Benjy was forced to soak his hand in Epsom salts.

By the end of the third week Mrs. Brabbam no longer came down to her mailbox. She didn't even come out the front door of her cabin to get the air, for Cora was always down at the road, leaning out, smiling for the mailman.

All too quickly the summer was at an end, or, at least, that part of the summer that counted most, anyway; Benjy's visit. There was his red bandanna hankerchief on the cabin table, sandwiches folded fresh and oniony in it, tied with a mint sprig to keep it clean to the smell; there on the floor, freshly polished, were his shoes to get into, and there on the chair, with his pencil which had once been long and yellow but was now stubby and chewed, sat Benjy. Cora took hold of his chin and tilted his head, as if she were testing a summer squash of an unfamiliar variety.

"Benjy, I owe you an apology. I don't think I looked at your face once in all this time. Seems I know every wart on your hand, every hangnail, every bump and every crinkle, but I might pass your face in a crowd and miss you."

"It's no face to look at," said Benjy shyly.

"But I'd know that hand in a million hands," Cora said. "Let anyone shake my hand in a dark room, a thousand people, and out of all those I'd say, 'Well, this one's Benjy.' " She smiled quietly and walked away to the open door. "I been thinking." She looked up at a distant cabin. "Ain't seen Mrs. Brabbam in weeks. Stays in all the time now. I've got a guilty feeling. I've done a prideful thing, a thing more sinful than she ever done me. I took the bottom out of her life. It was a mean and spiteful thing and I'm ashamed." She gazed up the hill toward that silent, locked place. "Benjy, would you do me one last favor?"

"Yes'm."

"Write a letter for Mrs. Brabbam."

"Ma'am?"

"Yes, write one of those companies for a free chart, a sample, something, and sign Mrs. Brabbam's name."

"All right," said Benjy.

"That way, in a week or a month the postman'll come by and whistle, and I'll tell him to go up to her door, special, and deliver it. And I'll be sure and be out in my front yard where I can see and Mrs. Brabbam can see I see. And I'll wave my letters to her and she'll wave her letters to me, and everybody'll smile."

"Yes'm," said Benjy.

He wrote three letters, licked the envelopes carefully, stuck them in his pocket. "I'll mail them when I get to St. Louis."

"It's been a fine summer," she said.

"It sure has."

"But, Benjy, I didn't learn to write, did I? I was after the letters and made you write late nights, and we were so busy sending labels and getting samples, land, it seemed there wasn't time to learn. And that means . . ."

He knew what it meant. He shook her hand. They stood in the cabin door. "Thanks," she said, "for everything."

Then he was running off. He ran as far as the meadow fence, leaped it easily, and the last she saw of him he was still running, waving the special letters, off into the great world over the hills.

The letters kept coming for some six months after Benjy went away. There would be the postman's little green car and the sharp ice-rimed shout of good morning, or the whistle, as he clapped two or three pink or blue envelopes into that fine mailbox.

And there was that special day when Mrs. Brabbam received her first real letter.

After that the letters were spaced a week apart, then a month, and finally the postman didn't say hello at all, there was no sound of a car coming up that lonely mountain road. First a spider moved into the mailbox, then a sparrow.

And Cora, while the letters still lasted, would clutch them in her bewildered hands, staring at them quietly until the pressure of her face muscles squeezed clear round shiny drops of water from her eyes. She'd hold up one blue envelope. "Who's this from?"

"Don't know," said Tom.

"What's it say?" she wailed.

"Don't know," said Tom.

"What's going on in that world out there, oh, I'll never know, I'll never know now," she said. "And this letter, and this one, and *this!*" She tumbled the stacks and stacks of letters that had come since Benjy ran off. "All the world and all the people and all the happenings, and me not knowing. All that world and people waiting to hear from us, and us not writing, and them not ever writing back!"

And at last the day came when the wind blew the mailbox over. In the mornings again, Cora would stand at the open door of her cabin, brushing her gray hair with a slow brush, not speaking, looking at the hills. And in all the years that followed she never passed the fallen mailbox without stooping aimlessly to fumble inside and take her hand out with nothing in it before she wandered on again into the fields.

15

POWERHOUSE

THE HORSES moved gently to a stop, and the man and his wife gazed down into a dry, sandy valley. The woman sat lost in her saddle; she hadn't spoken for hours, didn't know a good word to speak. She was trapped somewhere between the hot, dark pressure of the storm-clouded Arizona sky and the hard, granite pressure of the wind-blasted mountains. A few drops of cool rain fell on her trembling hands.

She looked over at her husband wearily. He sat his dusty horse easily, with a firm quietness. She closed her eyes and thought of how she had been all of these mild years until today. She wanted to laugh at the mirror she was holding up to herself, but there was no way of doing even that; it would be somewhat insane. After all, it might just be the pushing of this dark weather, or the telegram they had taken from the messenger on horseback this morning, or the long journey now to town.

There was still an empty world to cross, and she was cold.

"I'm the lady who was never going to need religion," she said quietly, her eyes shut.

"What?" Berty, her husband, glanced over at her.

"Nothing," she whispered, shaking her head. In all the years, how *certain* she had been. Never, never would she have need of a church. She had heard fine people talk on and on of religion and waxed pews and calla lilies in great bronze buckets and vast bells of churches in which the preacher rang like a clapper. She had heard the shouting kind and the fervent, whispery kind, and they were all the same. Hers was simply not a pew-shaped spine.

"I just never had a reason ever to sit in a church," she had told people. She wasn't vehement about it. She just walked around and lived and moved her hands that were pebble-smooth and pebble-small. Work had polished the nails of those hands with a polish you could never buy in a bottle. The touching of children had made them soft, and the raising of children had made them temperately stern, and the loving of a husband had made them gentle.

And now, death made them tremble.

"Here," said her husband. And the horses dusted down the trail to where an odd brick building stood beside a dry wash. The building was all glazed green windows, blue machinery, red tile, and wires. The wires ran off on high-tension towers to the farthest directions of the desert. She watched them go, silently, and, still held by her thoughts, turned her gaze back to the strange storm-green windows and the burning-colored bricks.

She had never slipped a ribbon in a Bible at a certain significant verse, because though her life in this desert was a life of granite, sun, and the steaming away of the waters of her flesh, there had never been a threat in it to her. Always things had worked out before the necessity had come for sleepless dawns and wrinkles in the forehead. Somehow, the very poisonous things of life had passed her. Death was a remote storm rumor beyond the farthest range.

Twenty years had blown in tumbleweeds, away, since she'd come West, worn this lonely trapping man's gold ring, and taken the desert as a third, and constant, partner to their living. None of their four children had ever been fearfully sick or near death. She had never had to get down on her knees except for the scrubbing of an already well-scrubbed floor.

Now all that was ended. Here they were riding toward a remote town because a simple piece of yellow paper had come and said very plainly that her mother was dying.

And she could not imagine it—no matter how she turned her head to see or turned her mind to look in on itself. There

112

were no rungs anywhere to hold to, going either up *or* down, and her mind like a compass left out in a sudden storm of sand, was suddenly blown free of all its once-clear directions, all points of reference worn away, the needle spinning without purpose, around, around. Even with Berty's arms on her back it wasn't enough. It was like the end of a good play and the beginning of an evil one. Someone she loved was actually going to die. This was impossible!

"I've got to stop," she said, not trusting her voice at all, so she made it sound irritated to cover her fear.

Berty knew her as no irritated woman, so the irritation did not carry over and fill him up. He was a capped jug; the contents there for sure. Rain on the outside didn't stir the brew. He side-ran his horse to her and took her hand gently. "Sure," he said. He squinted at the eastern sky. "Some clouds piling up black there. We'll wait a bit. It might rain. I wouldn't want to get caught in it."

Now she was irritated at her own irritation, one fed upon the other, and she was helpless. But rather than speak and risk the cycle's commencing again, she slumped forward and began to sob, allowing her horse to be led until it stood and tramped its feet softly beside the red brick building.

She slid down like a parcel into his arms, and he held her as she turned in on his shoulder; then he set her down and said, "Don't look like there's people here." He called, "Hey, there!" and looked at the sign on the door: *Danger. Bureau of Electric Power.*

There was a great insect humming all through the air. It sang in a ceaseless, bumbling tone, rising a bit, perhaps falling just a bit, but keeping the same pitch. Like a woman humming between pressed lips as she makes a meal in the warm twilight over a hot stove. They could see no movement within the building; there was only the gigantic humming. It was the sort of noise you would expect the sun-shimmer to make rising from hot railroad ties on a blazing summer day, when there is that flurried silence and you see the air eddy and whorl and ribbon, and expect a sound from the process but get nothing but an arched tautness of the eardrums and the tense quiet.

The humming came up through her heels, into her medium-slim legs, and thence to her body. It moved to her heart and touched it, as the sight of Berty just sitting on a top rail of the corral often did. And then it moved on to her head and the slenderest niches in the skull and set up a singing, as love songs and good books had done once on a time.

The humming was everywhere. It was as much a part of the soil as the cactus. It was as much a part of the air as the heat.

"What is it?" she asked, vaguely perplexed, looking at the building.

"I don't know much about it except it's a powerhouse," said Berty. He tried the door. "It's open," he said, surprised. "I wish someone was around." The door swung wide and the pulsing hum came out like a breath of air over them, louder.

They entered together into the solemn, singing place. She held him tightly, arm in arm.

It was a dim undersea place, smooth and clean and polished, as if something or other was always coming through and coming through and nothing ever stayed, but always there was motion and motion, invisible and stirring and never settling. On each side of them as they advanced were what first appeared to be people standing quietly, one after the other, in a double line. But these resolved into round, shell-like machines from which the humming sprang. Each black and gray and green machine gave forth golden cables and lime-colored wires, and there were silver metal pouches with crimson tabs and white lettering, and a pit like a washtub in which something whirled as if rinsing unseen materials at invisible speeds. The centrifuge raced so fast it stood still. Immense snakes of copper looped down from the twilight ceiling, and vertical pipes webbed up from cement floor to fiery brick wall. And the whole of it was as clean as a bolt of green lightning and smelled similarly. There was a crackling, eating sound, a dry rustling as of paper; flickers of blue fire shuttled, snapped, sparked, hissed where wires joined porcelain bobbins and green glass insulation.

Outside, in the real world, it began to rain.

She didn't want to stay in this place; it was no place to stay, with its people that were not people but dim machines and its music like an organ caught and pressed on a low note and a high note. But the rain washed every window and Berty said, "Looks like it'll last. Might have to stay the night here. It's late, anyhow. I'd better get the stuff in."

She said nothing. She wanted to be getting on. Getting on to what thing in what place, there was really no way of knowing. But at least in town she would hold onto the money and buy the tickets and hold them tight in her hand and hold onto a train which would rush and make a great noise, and get off the train, and get another horse, or get into a car hundreds of miles away and ride again, and stand at last by her dead or alive mother. It all depended on time and breath. There were many places she would pass through, but none of them would offer a thing to her except ground for her feet, air for her nostrils, food for her numb mouth. And these were worse than nothing. Why go to her mother at all,

114

say words, and make gestures? she wondered. What would be the use?

The floor was clean as a solid river under her. When she moved forward on it, it sent echoes cracking back and forth like small, faint gunshots through the room. Any word that was spoken came back as from a granite cavern.

Behind her, she heard Berty setting down the equipment. He spread two gray blankets and put out a little collection of tinned foods.

It was night. The rain still streamed on the high green-glazed windows, rinsing and making patterns of silk that flowed and intermingled in soft clear curtains. There were occasional thunderclaps which fell and broke upon themselves in avalanches of cold rain and wind hitting sand and stone.

Her head lay upon a folded cloth, and no matter how she turned it, the humming of the immense powerhouse worked up through the cloth into her head. She shifted, shut her eyes, and adjusted herself, but it went on and on. She sat up, patted the cloth, lay back down.

But the humming was there.

She knew without looking, by some sense deep in herself, that her husband was awake. There was no year she could remember when she hadn't known. It was some subtle difference in his breathing. It was the absence of sound, rather; no sound of breathing at all, save at long carefully thought-out intervals. She knew then that he was looking at her in the rainy darkness, concerned with her, taking great care of his breath.

She turned in the darkness. "Berty?"

"Yes?"

"I'm awake too," she said.

"I know," he said.

They lay, she very straight, very rigid, he in a half curl, like a hand relaxed, half bent inward. She traced this dark, easy curve and was filled with incomprehensible wonder.

"Berty," she asked, and paused a long while, "how . . . how are you like you are?"

He waited a moment. "How do you mean?" he said.

"How do you *rest*?" She stopped. It sounded very bad. It sounded so much like an accusation, but it was not, really. She knew him to be a man concerned with all things, a man who could see in darkness and who was not conceited because of his ability. He was worried for her now, and for her mother's life or death, but he had a way of worrying that seemed indifferent and irresponsible. It was neither of the two. His concern was all in him, deep; but it lay side by side with some faith, some belief that accepted it, made it welcome, and did not fight it. Something in him took hold of the sorrow first, got acquainted with it, knew each of its traceries before passing the message on to all of his waiting body. His body held a faith like a maze, and the sorrow that struck into him was lost and gone before it finally reached where it wanted to hurt him. Sometimes this faith drove her into a senseless anger, from which she recovered quickly, knowing how useless it was to criticize something as contained as a stone in a peach.

"Why didn't I ever catch it from you?" she said at last.

He laughed a little bit, softly. "Catch what?"

"I caught everything else. You shook me up and down in other ways. I didn't know anything but what you taught me." She stopped. It was hard to explain. Their life had been like the warm blood in a person passing through tissues quietly, both ways.

"Everything but religion," she said. "I never caught that from you."

"It's not a catching thing," he said. "Someday you just relax. And there it is."

Relax, she thought. Relax what? The body. But how to relax the mind? Her fingers twitched beside her. Her eyes wandered idly about the vast interior of the powerhouse. The machines stood over her in dark silhouettes with little sparkles crawling on them. The humming-humming-humming crept along her limbs.

Sleepy. Tired. She drowsed. Her eyes lidded and opened and lidded and opened. The humming-humming filled her marrow as if small hummingbirds were suspended in her body and in her head.

She traced the half-seen tubing up and up into the ceiling, and she saw the machines and heard the invisible whirlings. She suddenly became very alert in her drowsiness. Her eyes moved swiftly up and up and then down and across, and the humming-singing of the machines grew louder and louder, and her eyes moved, and her body relaxed; and on the tall, green windows she saw the shadows of the high-tension wires rushing off into the raining night.

Now the humming was in her, her eyes jerked, she felt herself yanked violently upright. She felt seized by a whirling dynamo, around, around and in a whirl, out, out, into the heart of whirling invisibilities, fed into, accepted by a thousand copper wires, and shot, in an instant, over the earth!

She was everywhere at once!

Streaking along high monster towers in instants, sizzling between high poles where small glass knobs sat like crystal-green birds holding the wires in their non-conductive beaks, branching in four directions, eight secondary directions, finding towns, hamlets, cities, racing on to farms, ranches, haciendas, she descended gently like a widely filamented spider web upon a thousand square miles of desert!

The earth was suddenly more than many separate things, more than houses, rocks, concrete roads, a horse here or there, a human in a shallow, boulder-topped grave, a prickling of cactus, a town invested with its own light surrounded by night, a million apart things. Suddenly it all had one pattern encompassed and held by the pulsing electric web.

She spilled out swiftly into rooms where life was rising from a slap on a naked child's back, into rooms where life was leaving bodies like the light fading from an electric bulb—the filament glowing, fading, finally colorless. She was in every town, every room, making light-patterns over hundreds of miles of land; seeing, hearing everything, not alone any more, but one of thousands of people, each with his ideas and his faiths.

Her body lay, a lifeless reed, pale and trembling. Her mind, in all its electric tensity, was flung about this way, that, down vast networks of powerhouse tributary.

Everything balanced. In one room she saw life wither; in another, a mile away, she saw wineglasses lifted to the newborn, cigars passed, smiles, handshakes, laughter. She saw the pale, drawn faces of people at white deathbeds, heard how they understood and accepted death, saw their gestures, felt their feelings, and saw that they, too, were lonely in themselves, with no way to get to the world to see the balance, see it as she was seeing it now.

She swallowed. Her eyelids flickered and her throat burned under her upraised fingers.

She was not alone.

The dynamo had whirled and flung her with centrifugal force out along a thousand lines into a million glass capsules screwed into ceilings, plucked into light by a pull of a cord or a twist of a knob or a flick of a switch.

The light could be in *any* room; all that was needed was to touch the switch. All rooms were dark until light came. And here she was, in all of them at once. And she was not alone. Her grief was but one part of a vast grief, her fear only one of countless others. And this grief was only a half thing. There was the other half; of things born, of comfort in the shape of a new child, of food in the warmed body, of colors for the eye and sounds in the awakened ear, and spring wild flowers for the smelling.

Whenever a light blinked out, life threw another switch; rooms were illumined afresh.

117

She was with those named Clark and those named Gray and the Shaws and Martins and Hanfords, the Fentons, the Drakes, the Shattucks, the Hubbells, and the Smiths. Being alone was not alone, except in the mind. You had all sorts of peekholes in your head. A silly, strange way to put it, perhaps, but there were the holes; the ones to see through and see that the world was there and people in it, as hard put to and uneasy as yourself; and there were the holes for hearing, and the one for speaking out your grief and getting rid of it, and the holes for knowing the changes of season through the scents of summer grain or winter ice or autumn fires. They were there to be used so that one was not alone. Loneliness was a shutting of the eyes. Faith was a simple opening.

The light-net fell upon all the world she had known for twenty years, herself blended with every line. She glowed and pulsed and was gentled in the great easy fabric. It lay across the land, covering each mile like a gentle, warm, and humming blanket. She was everywhere.

In the powerhouse the turbines whirled and hummed and the electric sparks, like little votive candles, jumped and clustered upon bent elbows of electric piping and glass. And the machines stood like saints and choruses, haloed now yellow, now red, now green, and a massed singing beat along the roof hollows and echoed down in endless hymns and chants. Outside, the wind clamored at the brick walls and drenched the glazed windows with rain; inside, she lay upon her small pillow and suddenly began to cry.

Whether it was with understanding, acceptance, joy, resignation, she couldn't know. The singing went on, higher and higher, and she was everywhere. She put out her hand, caught hold of her husband, who was still awake, his eyes fixed at the ceiling. Perhaps he had run everywhere, too, in this instant, through the network of light and power. But then, he had always been everywhere at once. He felt himself a unit of a whole and therefore he was stable; to her, unity was new and shaking. She felt his arms suddenly around her and she pressed her face into his shoulder for a long while, hard, while the humming and the humming climbed higher, and she cried freely, achingly, against him. . . .

In the morning the desert sky was very clear. They walked from the powerhouse quietly, saddled their horses, cinched on all of the equipment, and mounted.

She settled herself and sat there under the blue sky. And slowly she was aware of her back, and her back was straight, and she looked at her alien hands on the reins, and they had ceased trembling. And she could see the far mountains; there was no blur nor a running-of-color to things. All was solid stone touching stone, and stone touching sand, and sand touching wild flower, and wild flower touching the sky in one continuous clear flow, everything definite and of a piece.

"Wope!" cried Berty, and the horses walked slowly off, away from the brick building, through the cool sweet morning air.

She rode handsomely and she rode well, and in her, like a stone in a peach, was a peacefulness. She called to her husband as they slowed on a rise, "Berty!"

"Yes?"

"Can we . . ." she asked.

"Can we what?" he said, not hearing the first time.

"Can we come here again sometime?" she asked, nodding back toward the powerhouse. "Once in a while? Some Sunday?"

He looked at her and nodded slowly. "I reckon. Yes. Sure. I reckon so."

And as they rode on into town she was humming, humming a strange soft tune, and he glanced over and listened to it, and it was the sound you would expect to hear from sun-warmed railroad ties on a hot summer day when the air rises in a shimmer, flurried and whorling; a sound in one key, one pitch, rising a little, falling a little, humming, humming, but constant, peaceful, and wondrous to hear.

16

EN LA NOCHE

ALL NIGHT Mrs. Navarrez moaned, and these moans filled the tenement like a light turned on in every room so no one could sleep. All night she gnashed her white pillow and wrung her thin hands and cried, "My Joe!" The tenement people, at 3 A.M., finally discouraged that she would *never* shut her painted red mouth, arose, feeling warm and gritty, and dressed to take the trolley downtown to an all-night movie. There Roy Rogers chased bad men through veils of stale smoke and spoke dialogue above the soft snorings in the dark night theater.

By dawn Mrs. Navarrez was still sobbing and screaming.

During the day it was not so bad. Then the massed choir of babies crying here or there in the house added the saving grace of what was almost a harmony. There was also the chugging thunder of the washing machines on the tenement porch, and chenille-robed women standing on the flooded, soggy boards of the porch, talking their Mexican gossip rapidly. But now and again, above the shrill talk, the washing, the babies, one could

Copyright, 1952, by Fawcett Publications, Inc.

hear Mrs. Navarrez like a radio tuned high. "My Joe, oh, my poor Joe!" she screamed.

Now, at twilight, the men arrived with the sweat of their work under their arms. Lolling in cool bathtubs all through the cooking tenement, they cursed and held their hands to their ears.

"Is she *still* at it!" they raged helplessly. One man even kicked her door. "Shut *up*, woman!" But this only made Mrs. Navarrez shriek louder. "Oh, ah! Joe, Joe!"

"Tonight we eat out!" said the men to their wives. All through the house, kitchen utensils were shelved and doors locked as men hurried their perfumed wives down the halls by their pale elbows.

Mr. Villanazul, unlocking his ancient, flaking door at midnight, closed his brown eyes and stood for a moment, swaying. His wife Tina stood beside him with their three sons and two daughters, one in arms.

"Oh God," whispered Mr. Villanazul. "Sweet Jesus, come down off the cross and silence that woman." They entered their dim little room and looked at the blue candlelight flickering under a lonely crucifix. Mr. Villanazul shook his head philosophically. "He is still on the cross."

They lay in their beds like burning barbecues, the summer night basting them with their own liquors. The house flamed with that ill woman's cry.

"I am stifled!" Mr. Villanazul fled through the tenement, downstairs to the front porch with his wife, leaving the children, who had the great and miraculous talent of sleeping through all things.

Dim figures occupied the front porch, a dozen quiet men crouched with cigarettes fuming and glowing in their brown fingers, women in chenille wrappers taking what there was of the summer-night wind. They moved like dream figures, like clothes dummies worked stiffly on wires and rollers. Their eyes were puffed and their tongues thick.

"Let us go to her room and strangle her," said one of the men.

"No, that would not be right," said a woman. "Let us throw her from the window."

Everyone laughed tiredly.

Mr. Villanazul stood blinking bewilderedly at all the people. His wife moved sluggishly beside him.

"You would think Joe was the only man in the world to join the Army," someone said irritably. "Mrs. Navarrez, *pah!* This Joe-husband of hers will peel potatoes; the safest man in the infantry!"

"Something *must* be done." Mr. Villanazul had spoken. He was startled at the hard firmness of his own voice. Everyone glanced at him.

121

"We can't go on another night," Mr. Villanazul continued bluntly.

"The more we pound her door, the more she cries," explained Mr. Gomez.

"The priest came this afternoon," said Mrs. Gutierrez. "We sent for him in desperation. But Mrs. Navarrez would not even let him in the door, no matter how he pleaded. The priest went away. We had Officer Gilvie yell at her, too, but do you think she listened?"

"We must try some other way, then," mused Mr. Villanazul. "Someone must be—sympathetic—with her."

"What other way is there?" asked Mr. Gomez.

"If only," figured Mr. Villanazul after a moment's thought, "if only there was a *single* man among us."

He dropped that like a cold stone into a deep well. He let the splash occur and the ripples move gently out.

Everybody sighed.

It was like a little summer-night wind arisen. The men straightened up a bit; the women quickened.

"But," replied Mr. Gomez, sinking back, "we are all married. There is no single man."

"Oh," said everyone, and settled down into the hot, empty river bed of night, smoke rising, silent.

"Then," Mr. Villanazul shot back, lifting his shoulders, tightening his mouth, "it must be one of *us!*"

Again the night wind blew, stirring the people in awe.

"This is no time for selfishness!" declared Villanazul. "One of us must *do* this thing! That, or roast in hell another night!"

Now the people on the porch separated away from him, blinking. "*You* will do it, of course, Mr. Villanazul?" they wished to know.

He stiffened. The cigarette almost fell from his fingers. "Oh, but I——" he objected.

"You," they said. "Yes?"

He waved his hands feverishly. "I have a wife and five children, one in arms!"

"But none of us are single, and it is your idea and you must have the courage of your convictions, Mr. Villanazul!" everyone said.

He was very frightened and silent. He glanced with startled flashes of his eyes at his wife.

She stood wearily weaving on the night air, trying to see him.

"I'm so *tired*," she grieved.

"Tina," he said.

"I will die if I do not sleep," she said.

"Oh, but, Tina," he said.

"I will die and there will be many flowers and I will be buried if I do not get some rest," she murmured.

"She looks very bad," said everyone.

Mr. Villanazul hesitated only a moment longer. He touched his wife's slack hot fingers. He touched her hot cheek with his lips.

Without a word he walked from the porch.

They could hear his feet climbing the unlit stairs of the house, up and around to the third floor where Mrs. Navarrez wailed and screamed.

They waited on the porch.

The men lit new cigarettes and flicked away the matches, talking like the wind, the women wandering around among them, all of them coming and talking to Mrs. Villanazul, who stood, lines under her tired eyes, leaning against the porch rail.

"Now," whispered one of the men quietly. "Mr. Villanazul is at the top of the house!"

Everybody quieted.

"Now," hissed the man in a stage whisper. "Mr. Villanazul taps at her door! Tap, tap."

Everyone listened, holding his breath.

Far away there was a gentle tapping sound.

"Now, Mrs. Navarrez, at this intrusion, breaks out anew with crying!"

At the top of the house came a scream.

"Now," the man imagined, crouched, his hand delicately weaving on the air, "Mr. Villanazul pleads and pleads, softly, quietly, to the locked door."

The people on the porch lifted their chins tentatively, trying to see through three flights of wood and plaster to the third floor, waiting.

The screaming faded.

"Now, Mr. Villanazul talks quickly, he pleads, he whispers, he promises," cried the man softly.

The screaming settled to a sobbing, the sobbing to a moan, and finally all died away into breathing and the pounding of hearts and listening.

After about two minutes of standing, sweating, waiting, everyone on the porch heard the door far away upstairs rattle its lock, open, and, a second later, with a whisper, close.

The house was silent.

Silence lived in every room like a light turned off. Silence flowed like a cool wine in the tunnel halls. Silence came through the open casements like a cool breath from the cellar. They all stood breathing the coolness of it.

"Ah," they sighed.

Men flicked away cigarettes and moved on tiptoe into the silent tenement. Women followed. Soon the porch was empty. They drifted in cool halls of quietness.

Mrs. Villanazul, in a drugged stupor, unlocked her door.

123

"We must give Mr. Villanazul a banquet," a voice whispered. "Light a candle for him tomorrow."

The doors shut.

In her fresh bed Mrs. Villanazul lay. He is a thoughtful man, she dreamed, eyes closed. For such things, I love him.

The silence was like a cool hand, stroking her to sleep.

17

SUN AND SHADOW

THE CAMERA clicked like an insect. It was blue and metallic, like a great fat beetle held in the man's precious and tenderly exploiting hands. It winked in the flashing sunlight.

"Hsst, Ricardo, come away!"

"You down there!" cried Ricardo out the window.

"Ricardo, stop!"

He turned to his wife. "Don't tell me to stop, tell them to stop. Go down and tell them, or are you afraid?"

"They aren't hurting anything," said his wife patiently.

He shook her off and leaned out the window and looked down into the alley. "You there!" he cried.

The man with the black camera in the alley glanced up, then went on focusing his machine at the lady in the salt-white beach pants, the white bra, and the green checkered scarf. She leaned against the cracked plaster of the building. Behind her a dark boy smiled, his hand to his mouth.

"Tomás!" yelled Ricardo. He turned to his wife. "Oh, Jesus

the Blessed, Tomás is in the street, my own son laughing there."
Ricardo started out the door.

"Don't do anything!" said his wife.

"I'll cut off their heads!" said Ricardo, and was gone.

In the street the lazy woman was lounging now against the peeling blue paint of a banister. Ricardo emerged in time to see her doing this. "That's my banister!" he said.

The cameraman hurried up. "No, no, we're taking pictures. Everything's all right. We'll be moving on."

"Everything's not all right," said Ricardo, his brown eyes flashing. He waved a wrinkled hand. "She's on my house."

"We're taking fashion pictures," smiled the photographer.

"*Now* what am I to do?" said Ricardo to the blue sky. "Go mad with this news? Dance around like an epileptic saint?"

"If it's money, well, here's a five-peso bill," smiled the photographer.

Ricardo pushed the hand away. "I *work* for my money. You don't understand. Please go."

The photographer was bewildered. "Wait . . ."

"Tomás, get in the house!"

"But, Papa . . ."

"Gahh!" bellowed Ricardo.

The boy vanished.

"This has *never* happened before," said the photographer.

"It is long past time! What are we? Cowards?" Ricardo asked the world.

A crowd was gathering. They murmured and smiled and nudged each other's elbows. The photographer with irritable good will snapped his camera shut, said over his shoulder to the model, "All right, we'll use that other street. I saw a nice cracked wall there and some nice deep shadows. If we hurry . . ."

The girl, who had stood during this exchange nervously twisting her scarf, now seized her make-up kit and darted by Ricardo, but not before he touched at her arm. "Do not misunderstand," he said quickly. She stopped, blinked at him. He went on. "It is not you I am mad at. Or you." He addressed the photographer.

"Then why——" said the photographer.

Ricardo waved his hand. "You are employed; I am employed. We are all people employed. We must understand each other. But when you come to my house with your camera that looks like the complex eye of a black horsefly, then the understanding is over. I will not have my alley used because of its pretty shadows, or my sky used because of its sun, or my house used because there is an interesting crack in the wall, here! You *see!* Ah, how beautiful! Lean here! Stand there! Sit here!

Crouch there! Hold it! Oh, I *heard* you. Do you think I am stupid? I have books up in my room. You see that window? Maria!"

His wife's head popped out. "Show them my books!" he cried.

She fussed and muttered, but a moment later she held out one, then two, then half a dozen books, eyes shut, head turned away, as if they were old fish.

"And two dozen more like them upstairs!" cried Ricardo. "You're not talking to some cow in the forest, you're talking to a man!"

"Look," said the photographer, packing his plates swiftly. "We're going. Thanks for nothing."

"Before you go, you must see what I am getting at," said Ricardo. "I am not a mean man. But I *can* be a very angry man. Do I look like a cardboard cutout?"

"Nobody said anybody looked like anything." The photographer hefted his case and started off.

"There is a photographer two blocks over," said Ricardo, pacing him. "They have cutouts. You stand in front of them. It says 'GRAND HOTEL.' They take a picture of you and it looks like you are in the Grand Hotel. Do you see what I mean? My alley is my alley, my life is my life, my son is my son. My son is not cardboard! I saw you putting my son against the wall, so, and thus, in the background. What do you call it—for the correct air? To make the whole attractive, and the lovely lady in front of him?"

"It's getting late," said the photographer, sweating. The model trotted along on the other side of him.

"We are poor people," said Ricardo. "Our doors peel paint, our walls are chipped and cracked, our gutters fume in the street, the alleys are all cobbles. But it fills me with a terrible rage when I see you make over these things as if I had *planned* it this way, as if I had years ago induced the wall to crack. Did you think I knew you were coming and aged the paint? Or that I knew you were coming and put my boy in his dirtiest clothes? We are *not* a studio! We are people and must be given attention as people. Have I made it clear?"

"With abundant detail," said the photographer, not looking at him, hurrying.

"Now that you know my wishes and my reasoning, you will do the friendly thing and go home?"

"You are a hilarious man," said the photographer. "Hey!" They had joined a group of five other models and a second photographer at the base of a vast stone stairway which in layers, like a bridal cake, led up to the white town square. "How you doing, Joe?"

"We got some beautiful shots near the Church of the Virgin, some statuary without any noses, lovely stuff," said Joe. "What's the commotion?"

"Pancho here got in an uproar. Seems we leaned against his house and knocked it down."

"My name is Ricardo. My house is completely intact."

"We'll shoot it *here*, dear," said the first photographer. "Stand by the archway of that store. There's a nice antique wall going up there." He peered into the mysteries of his camera.

"So!" A dreadful quiet came upon Ricardo. He watched them prepare. When they were ready to take the picture he hurried forward, calling to a man in a doorway. "Jorge! What are you *doing?*"

"I'm standing here," said the man.

"Well," said Ricardo, "isn't that *your* archway? Are you going to let them *use* it?"

"I'm not bothered," said Jorge.

Ricardo shook his arm. "They're treating your property like a movie actor's place. Aren't you insulted?"

"I haven't thought about it." Jorge picked his nose.

"Jesus upon earth, man, *think!*"

"I can't see any harm," said Jorge.

"Am I the *only* one in the world with a tongue in my mouth?" said Ricardo to his empty hands. "And taste on my tongue? Is this a town of backdrops and picture sets? Won't *anyone* do something about this except me?"

The crowd had followed them down the street, gathering others to it as it came; now it was of a fair size and more were coming, drawn by Ricardo's bullish shouts. He stomped his feet. He made fists. He spat. The cameraman and the models watched him nervously. "Do you want a *quaint* man in the background?" he said wildly to the cameraman. "I'll pose back here. Do you want me near this wall, my hat *so*, my feet *so*, the light so and thus on my sandals which I made myself? Do you want me to rip this hole in my shirt a bit larger, eh, like *this? So!* Is my face smeared with enough perspiration? Is my hair long enough, kind sir?"

"Stand there if you want," said the photographer.

"I won't look in the camera," Ricardo assured him.

The photographer smiled and lifted his machine. "Over to your left one step, dear." The model moved. "Now turn your right leg. That's fine. Fine, fine. *Hold* it!"

The model froze, chin tilted up.

Ricardo dropped his pants.

"Oh, my God!" said the photographer.

Some of the models squealed. The crowd laughed and pummeled each other a bit. Ricardo quietly raised his pants and leaned against the wall.

"Was that quaint enough?" he said.

"Oh, my God!" muttered the photographer.

"Let's go down to the docks," said his assistant.

"I think *I'll* go there too," Ricardo smiled.

"Good God, what can we do with the idiot?" whispered the photographer.

"Buy him off!"

"I *tried* that!"

"You didn't go high enough."

"Listen, you run get a policeman. I'll put a stop to this."

The assistant ran. Everyone stood around smoking cigarettes nervously, eying Ricardo. A dog came by and briefly made water against the wall.

"Look at that!" cried Ricardo. "What art! What a pattern! Quick, before the sun dries it!"

The cameraman turned his back and looked out to sea.

The assistant came rushing along the street. Behind him, a native policeman strolled quietly. The assistant had to stop and run back to urge the policeman to hurry. The policeman assured him with a gesture, at a distance, that the day was not yet over and in time they would arrive at the scene of whatever disaster lay ahead.

The policeman took up a position behind the two cameramen. "What seems to be the trouble?"

"That man up there. We want him removed."

"That man up there seems only to be leaning against a wall," said the officer.

"No, no, it's not the leaning, he—— Oh hell," said the cameraman. "The only way to explain is to show you. Take your pose, dear."

The girl posed. Ricardo posed, smiling casually.

"Hold it!"

The girl froze.

Ricardo dropped his pants.

Click went the camera.

"Ah," said the policeman.

"Got the evidence right in this old camera if you need it!" said the cameraman.

"Ah," said the policeman, not moving, hand to chin. "So." He surveyed the scene like an amateur photographer himself. He saw the model with the flushed, nervous marble face, the cobbles, the wall, and Ricardo. Ricardo magnificently smoking a cigarette there in the noon sunlight under the blue sky, his pants where a man's pants rarely are.

"Well, officer?" said the cameraman, waiting.

"Just what," said the policeman, taking off his cap and wiping his dark brow, "do you want me to do?"

"Arrest that man! Indecent exposure!"

"Ah," said the policeman.

"Well?" said the cameraman.

The crowd murmured. All the nice lady models were looking out at the sea gulls and the ocean.

"That man up there against the wall," said the officer, "I know him. His name is Ricardo Reyes."

"Hello, Esteban!" called Ricardo.

The officer called back at him, "Hello, Ricardo."

They waved at each other.

"He's not doing anything *I* can see," said the officer.

"What do you mean?" asked the cameraman. "He's as naked as a rock. It's immoral!"

"That man is doing nothing immoral. He's just standing there," said the policeman. "Now if he were *doing* something with his hands or body, something terrible to view, I would act upon the instant. However, since he is simply leaning against the wall, not moving a single limb or muscle, there *is* nothing wrong."

"He's naked, *naked!*" screamed the cameraman.

"I don't understand." The officer blinked.

"You just don't go around naked, that's all!"

"There are naked people and naked people," said the officer. "Good and bad. Sober and with drink in them. I judge this one to be a man with no drink in him, a good man by reputation; naked, yes, but doing nothing with this nakedness in any way to offend the community."

"What *are* you, his *brother?* What are you, his confederate?" said the cameraman. It seemed that at any moment he might snap and bite and bark and woof and race around in circles under the blazing sun. "Where's the justice? What's going *on* here? Come on, girls, we'll go somewhere else!"

"France," said Ricardo.

"What!" The photographer whirled.

"I said France, or Spain," suggested Ricardo. "Or Sweden. I have seen some nice pictures of walls in Sweden. But not many cracks in them. Forgive my suggestion."

"We'll get pictures in spite of you!" The cameraman shook his camera, his fist.

"I will be there," said Ricardo. "Tomorrow, the next day, at the bullfights, at the market, anywhere, everywhere you go I go, quietly, with grace. With dignity, to perform my necessary task."

Looking at him, they knew it was true.

"Who are you—who in hell do you think you are?" cried the photographer.

"I have been waiting for you to ask me," said Ricardo. "Consider me. Go home and think of me. As long as there is

130

one man like me in a town of ten thousand, the world will go on. Without me, all would be chaos."

"Good night, nurse," said the photographer, and the entire swarm of ladies, hatboxes, cameras, and make-up kits retreated down the street toward the docks. "Time out for lunch, dears. We'll figure something later!"

Ricardo watched them go, quietly. He had not moved from his position. The crowd still looked upon him and smiled.

Now, Ricardo thought, I will walk up the street to my house, which has paint peeling from the door where I have brushed it a thousand times in passing, and I shall walk over the stones I have worn down in forty-six years of walking, and I shall run my hand over the crack in the wall of my own house, which is the crack made by the earthquake in 1930. I remember well the night, us all in bed, Tomás as yet unborn, and Maria and I much in love, and thinking it was our love which moved the house, warm and great in the night; but it was the earth trembling, and in the morning, that crack in the wall. And I shall climb the steps to the lacework-grille balcony of my father's house, which grillwork he made with his own hands, and I shall eat the food my wife serves me on the balcony, with the books near at hand. And my son Tomás, whom I created out of whole cloth, yes, bed sheets, let us admit it, with my good wife. And we shall sit eating and talking, not photographs, not backdrops, not paintings, not stage furniture, any of us. But actors, all of us, very fine actors indeed.

As if to second this last thought, a sound startled his ear. He was in the midst of solemnly, with great dignity and grace, lifting his pants to belt them around his waist, when he heard this lovely sound. It was like the winging of soft doves in the air. It was applause.

The small crowd, looking up at him, enacting the final scene of the play before the intermission for lunch, saw with what beauty and gentlemanly decorum he was elevating his trousers. The applause broke like a brief wave upon the shore of the nearby sea.

Ricardo gestured and smiled to them all.

On his way home up the hill he shook hands with the dog that had watered the wall.

18

THE MEADOW

A WALL COLLAPSES, followed by another and another; with dull thunder, a city falls into ruin.

The night wind blows.

The world lies silent.

London was torn down during the day. Port Said was destroyed. The nails were pulled out of San Francisco. Glasgow is no more.

They are gone, forever.

Boards clatter softly in the wind, sand whines and trickles in small storms upon the still air.

Along the road toward the colorless ruins comes the old night watchman to unlock the gate in the high barbed-wire fence and stand looking in.

There in the moonlight lie Alexandria and Moscow and New York. There in the moonlight lie Johannesburg and Dublin and Stockholm. And Clearwater, Kansas, and Provincetown, and Rio de Janeiro.

Just this afternoon the old man saw it happen, saw the car

Copyright, 1947, by Dodd, Mead & Co., Inc.

roaring outside the barbed-wire fence, saw the lean, sun-tanned men in that car, the men with their luxurious charcoal-flannel suits, and winking gold-mask cuff links, and their burning-gold wrist watches, and eye-blinding rings, lighting their cork-tipped cigarettes with engraved lighters. . . .

"There it is, gentlemen. What a mess. Look what the weather's done to it."

"Yes, sir, it's bad, Mr. Douglas!"

"We just *might* save Paris."

"Yes, *sir!*"

"But, hell! The rain's warped it. That's Hollywood for you! Tear it down! Clear it out! We can use that land. Send a wrecking crew in today!"

"Yes, *sir,* Mr. Douglas!"

The car roaring off and gone away.

And now it is night. And the old night watchman stands inside the gate.

He remembers what happened this same still afternoon when the wreckers came.

A hammering, ripping, clattering; a collapse and a roar. Dust and thunder, thunder and dust!

And the whole of the entire world shook loose its nails and lath and plaster and sill and celluloid window as town after town following town banged over flat and lay still.

A shuddering, a thunder fading away, and then, once more, only the quiet wind.

The night watchman now walks slowly forward along the empty streets.

And one moment he is in Baghdad, and beggars loll in wondrous filth, and women with clear sapphire eyes give veiled smiles from high thin windows.

The wind blows sand and confetti.

The women and beggars vanish.

And it is all strutworks again, it is all papier-mâché and oil-painted canvas and props lettered with the name of this studio, and there is nothing behind any of the building fronts but night and space and stars.

The old man pulls a hammer and a few long nails from his tool chest; he peers around in the junk until he finds a dozen good strong boards and some untorn canvas. And he takes the bright steel nails in his blunt fingers, and they are single-headed nails.

And he begins to put London back together again, hammering and hammering, board by board, wall by wall, window by window, hammering, hammering, louder, louder, steel on steel, steel in wood, wood against sky, working the hours toward midnight, with no end to his striking and fixing and striking again.

"Hey there, *you!*"

The old man pauses.

"You, night *watchman!*"

Out of the shadows hurries a stranger in overalls, calling: "Hey, what's-your-name!"

The old man turns. "The name's Smith."

"Okay, Smith, what in hell's the idea!"

The watchman eyes the stranger quietly. "Who are *you?*"

"Kelly, foreman of the wrecking gang."

The old man nods. "Ah. The ones who tear everything down. You've done plenty today. Why aren't you home bragging about it?"

Kelly hawks and spits. "There was some machinery over on the Singapore set I had to check." He wipes his mouth. . . . "Now, Smith, what in Christ's name you think you're doing? Drop that hammer. You're building it all up again! We tear it down and you put it up. You crazy?"

The old man nods. "Maybe I am. But somebody has to put it up again."

"Look, Smith. I do *my* work, you do yours, everyone's happy. But I can't have you messing, see? I'm turning you in to Mr. Douglas."

The old man goes on with his hammering. "Call him up. Send him around. I want to talk to him. *He's* the crazy one."

Kelly laughs. "You kidding? Douglas don't see nobody." He jerks his hand, then bends to examine Smith's newly finished work. "Hey, wait a minute! What *kind* of nails you using? Single-heads! Now, *cut that!* It'll be hell to pay tomorrow, trying to pull 'em out!"

Smith turns his head and looks for a moment at the other man swaying there. "Well, it stands to reason you can't put the world together with double-headed nails. They're too easy to yank out. You got to use single-headed nails and hammer 'em way in. Like *this!*"

He gives a steel nail one tremendous blow that buries it completely in the wood.

Kelly works his hands on his hips. "I'll give you one more chance. Quit putting things back together and I'll play ball with you."

"Young man," says the night watchman, and keeps on hammering while he talks, and thinks about it, and talks some more, "I was here long before you were born. I was here when all *this* was only a meadow. And there was a wind set the meadow running in waves. For more than thirty years I watched it grow, until it was all of the world together. I lived here *with* it. I lived nice. This is the *real* world to me now. That world out there, beyond the fence, is where I spend time sleeping. I got a little room on a little street, and I see headlines and read about wars

134

and strange, bad people. But here? Here I have the whole world together and it's all peace. I been walking through the cities of *this* world since 1920. Any night I feel like it, I have a one-o'clock snack at a bar on the Champs Elysées! I can get me some fine amontillado sherry at a sidewalk café in Madrid, if I want. Or else me and the stone gargoyles, high up there—you *see* them, on top Notra Dame?—we can turn over great state matters and reach big political decisions!"

"Yeah, Pop, sure." Kelly waves impatiently.

"And now you come and kick it down and leave only that world out there which hasn't learned the *first thing* about peace that I know from seeing this land here inside the barbed wire. And so you come and rip it up and there's no peace any more, anywhere. You and your wreckers so proud of your wrecking. Pulling down towns and cities and whole lands!"

"A guy's got to live," says Kelly. "I got a wife and kids."

"That's what they all say. They got wives and kids. And they go on, pulling apart, tearing down, killing. They had *orders!* Somebody *told* them. They *had* to do it!"

"Shut up and gimme that hammer!"

"Don't come any closer!"

"Why, you crazy old——"

"This hammer's good for more than nails!" The old man whistles the hammer through the air; the wrecker jumps back.

"Hell," says Kelly, "you're insane! I'm putting a call through to the main studio; we'll get some cops here quick. My God, one minute you're building things up and talking crazy, but how do I know two minutes from now you won't run wild and start pouring kerosene and lighting matches!"

"I wouldn't harm the smallest piece of kindling in this place, and you know it," says the old man.

"Might burn the whole goddam place down, hell," says Kelly. "Listen, old man, you just wait right *there!*"

The wrecker spins about and runs off into the villages and the ruined cities and the sleeping two-dimensional towns of this night world, and after his footsteps fade there is a music that the wind plays on the long silver barbed wires of the fence, and the old man hammering and hammering and selecting long boards and rearing walls until a time finally comes when his mouth is gasping, his heart is exploding; the hammer drops from his open fingers, steel nails tinkle like coins on the pavement, and the old man cries out to himself alone:

"It's no use, no use. I can't put it all back up before they come. I need so very much help I don't know what to do."

The old man leaves his hammer lying on the road and begins to walk with no direction, with no purpose, it seems, save that he is thinking to make one last round and take one last look at everything and say good-by to whatever there is or was in this

135

world to say good-by to. And so he walks with the shadows all around and the shadows all through this land where time has grown late indeed, and the shadows are of all kinds and types and sizes, shadows of buildings, and shadows of people. And he doesn't look straight *at* them, no, because if he looked at them straight, they would all blow away. No, he just walks, down the middle of Piccadilly Circus . . . the echo of his steps . . . or the Rue de la Paix . . . the sound of him clearing his throat . . . or Fifth Avenue . . . and he doesn't look right or left. And all around him, in dark doorways and empty windows, are his many friends, his good friends, his *very* good friends. Far away there are the hiss and steam and soft whispering of a *caffè espresso* machine, all silver and chrome, and soft Italian singing . . . the flutter of hands in darkness over the open mouths of balalaikas, the rustle of palm trees, a touching of drums with the chimes chiming and small bells belling, and a sound of summer apples dropped in soft night grass which are not apples at all but the motion of women's bared feet slowly dancing a circle to the chimes' faint chiming and the belling of the tiny golden bells. There is the munch of maize kernels crushed on black volcanic stone, the sizzle of tortillas drowned in hot fat, the whisk of charcoals tossing up a thousand fireflies of spark at the blowing of a mouth and the wave of a papaya frond; everywhere faces and forms, everywhere stirs and gestures and ghost fires which float the magical torch-colored faces of Spanish gypsies in air as on a fiery water, the mouths crying out the songs that tell of the oddness and the strangeness and the sadness of living. Everywhere shadows and people, everywhere people and shadows and singing to music.

Just that very trite thing—the wind?

No. The people are all here. They have been here for many years. And tomorrow?

The old man stops, presses his hands to his chest.

They will not be here any more.

A horn blows!

Outside the barbed-wire gate—the enemy! Outside the gate a small black police car and a large black limousine from the studio itself, three miles away.

The horn blares!

The old man seizes the rungs of a ladder and climbs, the sound of the horn pushing him higher and higher. The gate crashes wide; the enemy roars in.

"There he goes!"

The glaring lights of the police shine in upon the cities of the meadow; the lights reveal the stark canvas set-pieces of Manhattan, Chicago, and Chungking! The light glitters on the imitation stone towers of Notre Dame Cathedral, fixes on a tiny figure balancing on the catwalks of Notre Dame, climbing and climbing up where the night and the stars are turning slowly by.

"There he is, Mr. Douglas, at the top!"

"Good God. It's getting so a man can't spend an evening at a quiet party without——"

"He's striking a match! Call the fire department!"

On top of Notre Dame, the night watchman, looking down, shielding the match from the softly blowing wind, sees the police, the workmen, and the producer in a dark suit, a big man, gazing up at him. Then the night watchman slowly turns the match, cupping it, applies it to the tip of his cigar. He lights the cigar in slow puffs.

He calls: "Is Mr. Douglas down there?"

A voice calls back: "What do you want with me?"

The old man smiles. "Come up, alone! Bring a gun if you want! I just want a little talk!"

The voices echo in the vast churchyard:

"Don't *do* it, Mr. Douglas!"

"Give me your gun. Let's get this *over* with so I can get back to the party. Keep me covered, I'll play it safe. I don't want these sets burned. There's two million dollars in lumber alone here. *Ready?* I'm on my way."

The producer climbs high on the night ladders, up through the half shell of Notre Dame to where the old man leans against a plaster gargoyle, quietly smoking a cigar. The producer stops, gun pointed, half through an open trap door.

"All right, Smith. Stay where you are."

Smith removes the cigar from his mouth quietly. "Don't you be afraid of me. I'm all right."

"I wouldn't bet money on that."

"Mr. Douglas," says the night watchman, "did you ever read that story about the man who traveled to the future and found everyone there insane? *Everyone.* But since they were all insane they didn't *know* they were insane. They all acted alike and so they thought themselves normal. And since our hero was the only sane one among them, he was abnormal; therefore, *he* was the insane one. To *them,* at least. Yes, Mr. Douglas, insanity is relative. It depends on who has who locked in what cage."

The producer swears under his breath. "I didn't climb up here to talk all night. What do you want?"

"I want to talk with the Creator. That's you, Mr. Douglas. You created all this. You came here one day and struck the earth with a magical checkbook and cried, 'Let there be Paris!' And there *was* Paris: streets, bistros, flowers, wine, outdoor bookshops and all. And you clapped your hands again: 'Let there be Constantinople!' And there *it* was! You clapped your hands a thousand times, and each time made something new, and now you think just by clapping your hands one *last* time you can drop it all down in ruins. But, Mr. Douglas, it's not as easy as that!"

"I own fifty-one per cent of the stock in this studio!"

"But did the studio ever belong to you, really? Did you ever think to drive here late some night and climb up on this cathedral and see what a *wonderful* world you created? Did you ever wonder if it might not be a good idea for you to sit up here with me and my friends and have a cup of amontillado sherry with us? All right—so the amontillado smells and looks and tastes like coffee. Imagination, Mr. Creator, imagination. But no, you never came around, you never climbed up, you never looked or listened or cared. There was always a party somewhere else. And now, very late, without asking us, you want to destroy it all. You may own fifty-one per cent of the studio stock, but you don't own *them*."

"Them!" cries the producer. "What's all this business about 'them'?"

"It's hard to put in words. The people who *live* here." The night watchman moves his hand in the empty air toward the half cities and the night. "So many films were made here in all the long years. Extras moved in the streets in costumes, they talked a thousand tongues, they smoked cigarettes and meerschaums and Persian hookahs, even. Dancing girls danced. They *glittered*, oh, how they glittered! Women with veils smiled down from high balconies. Soldiers marched. Children played. Knights in silver armor fought. There were orange-tea shops. People sipped tea in them and dropped their *h*'s. Gongs were beaten. Viking ships sailed the inland seas."

The producer lifts himself up through the trap door and sits on the plankings, the gun cradled more easily in his hand. He seems to be looking at the old man first with one eye, then the other, listening to him with one ear, then the other, shaking his head a little to himself.

The night watchman continues:

"And somehow, after the extras and the men with the cameras and microphones and all the equipment walked away and the gates were shut and they drove off in big cars, somehow something of all those thousands of different people remained. The things they had been, or *pretended* to be, stayed on. The foreign languages, the costumes, the things they did, the things they thought about, their religions and their music, all those little things and big things stayed on. The sights of far places. The smells. The salt wind. The sea. It's all here tonight—if you *listen*."

The producer listens and the old man listens in the drafty strutworks of the cathedral, with the moonlight blinding the eyes of the plaster gargoyles and the wind making the false stone mouths to whisper, and the sound of a thousand lands within a land below blowing and dusting and leaning in that wind, a thousand yellow minarets and milk-white towers and green avenues yet untouched among the hundred new ruins, and all of it murmuring its wires and lathings like a great steel-and-wooden harp touched in the night, and the wind bringing that self-made sound high up here in the sky to these two men who stand listening and apart.

The producer laughs shortly and shakes his head.

"You *heard,*" says the night watchman. "You *did* hear, didn't you? I see it in your face."

Douglas shoves the gun in his coat pocket. "Anything you listen for you can hear. I made the mistake of listening. You should have been a writer. You could throw six of my best ones out of work. Well, what about it—are you ready to come down out of here now?"

"You sound almost polite," says the night watchman.

"Don't know why I should. You ruined a good evening for me."

"Did I? It hasn't been that bad, has it? A bit different, I should say. Stimulating, maybe."

Douglas laughs quietly. "You're not dangerous at all. You just need company. It's your job and everything going to hell and you're lonely. I can't quite figure you, though."

"Don't tell me I've got you thinking?" asks the old man.

Douglas snorts. "After you've lived in Hollywood long enough, you meet all kinds. Besides, I've never been up here before. It's a real view, like you say. But I'll be damned if I can figure why you should worry about all this junk. What's it to you?"

The night watchman gets down on one knee and taps one hand into the palm of the other, illustrating his points. "Look. As I said before, you came here years ago, clapped your hands, and three hundred cities jumped up! Then you added a half thousand other nations, and states and peoples and religions and political setups inside the barbed-wire fence. And there was trouble! Oh, nothing you could see. It was all in the wind and the spaces between. But it was the same kind of trouble the world out there beyond the fence has—squabbles and riots and invisible wars. But at last the trouble died out. You want to know why?"

"If I didn't, I wouldn't be sitting up here freezing."

A little night music, please, thinks the old man, and moves his hand on the air like someone playing the proper and beautiful music to background all that he has to tell. . . .

"Because you got Boston joined to Trinidad," he says softly, "part of Trinidad poking out of Lisbon, part of Lisbon leaning on Alexandria, Alexandria tacked onto Shanghai, and a lot of little pegs and nails between, like Chattanooga, Oshkosh, Oslo,

Sweet Water, Soissons, Beirut, Bombay, and Port Arthur. You shoot a man in New York and he stumbles forward and drops dead in Athens. You take a political bribe in Chicago and somebody in London goes to jail. You hang a Negro man in Alabama and the people of Hungary have to bury him. The dead Jews of Poland clutter the streets of Sydney, Portland, and Tokyo. You push a knife into a man's stomach in Berlin and it comes out the back of a farmer in Memphis. It's all so *close,* so very *close.* That's why we have peace here. We're all so crowded there *has got to be peace,* or nothing would be left! One fire would destroy all of us, no matter who started it, for what reason. So all of the people, the memories, whatever you want to call them, that are here, have settled down, and this is their world, a good world, a fine world."

The old man stops and licks his lips slowly and takes a breath. "And tomorrow," he says, "you're going to stomp it down."

The old man crouches there a moment longer, then gets to his feet and gazes out at the cities and the thousand shadows in those cities. The great plaster cathedral whines and sways in the night air, back and forth, rocking on the summer tides.

"Well," says Douglas at last, "shall—shall we go down now?"

Smith nods. "I've had my say."

Douglas vanishes, and the watchman listens to the younger man going down and down through the ladders and catwalks of the night. Then, after a reasonable hesitation, the old man takes hold of the ladder, breathes something to himself, and begins the long descent in shadow.

The studio police and the few workers and some minor executives all drive away. Only one large dark car waits outside the barbed-wire gate as the two men stand talking in the cities of the meadow.

"What are you going to do now?" asks Smith.

"Go back to my party, I suppose," says the producer.

"Will it be fun?"

"Yes." The producer hesitates. "Sure, it'll be fun!" He glances at the night watchman's right hand. "Don't tell me you've found that hammer Kelly told me you were using? You going to start building again? You don't give up, do you?"

"Would you, if you were the last builder and everybody else was a wrecker?"

Douglas starts to walk with the old man. "Well, maybe I'll see you again, Smith."

"No," says Smith, "I won't be here. This all won't be here. If you come back again, it'll be too late."

Douglas stops. "Hell, hell! What do you want me to do?"

"A simple thing. Leave all this standing. Leave these cities up."

"I can't do that! Damn it. Business reasons. It has to go."

"A man with a real nose for business and some imagination could think up a profitable reason for it to stay," says Smith.

"My car's waiting! How do I get out of here?"

The producer strikes off over a patch of rubble, cuts through half of a tumbled ruin, kicking boards aside, leaning for a moment on plaster façades and strutworks. Dust rains from the sky.

"Watch out!"

The producer stumbles in a thunder of dust and avalanching brick; he gropes, he topples, he is seized upon by the old man and yanked forward.

"Jump!"

They jump, and half the building slides to ruin, crashes into hills and mountains of old paper and lathing. A great bloom of dust strikes out upon the air.

"You all right?"

"Yes. Thanks. Thanks." The producer looks at the fallen building. The dust clears. "You probably saved my life."

"Hardly that. Most of those are papier-mâché bricks. You might have been cut and bruised a little."

"Nevertheless, thanks. What building was that that fell?"

"Norman village tower, built in 1925. Don't get near the rest of it; it might go down."

"I'll be careful." The producer moves carefully in to stand by the set-piece. "Why—I could push this whole damn building over with one hand." He demonstrates; the building leans and quivers and groans. The producer steps quickly back. "I could knock it down in a second."

"But you wouldn't want to do that," says the watchman.

"Oh, wouldn't I? What's one French house more or less, this late in the day?"

The old man takes his arm. "Walk around here to the other side of the house."

They walk to the other side.

"Read that sign," says Smith.

The producer flicks his cigarette lighter, holds the fire up to help him squint, and reads:

" 'THE FIRST NATIONAL BANK, MELLIN TOWN.' " He pauses. " 'ILLINOIS,' " he says, very slowly.

The building stands there in the sharp light of the stars and the bland light of the moon.

"On one side"—Douglas balances his hand like a scales—"a French tower. On the other side——" He walks seven steps to the right, seven steps to the left, peering. " 'THE FIRST NATIONAL BANK.' Bank. Tower. Tower. Bank. Well, I'll be *damned*."

Smith smiles and says, "Still want to push the French tower down, Mr. Douglas?"

"Wait a minute, wait a minute, hold on, hold on," says Douglas, and suddenly begins to see the buildings that stand before him. He turns in a slow circle; his eyes move up and down and across and over; his eyes flick here, flick there, see this, see that, examine, file, put away, and re-examine. He begins to walk in silence. They move in the cities of the meadow, over grasses and wild flowers, up to and into and through ruins and half ruins and up to and into and through complete avenues and villages and towns.

They begin a recital which goes on and on as they walk, Douglas asking, the night watchman answering, Douglas asking, the night watchman answering.

"What's this over here?"

"A Buddhist temple."

"And on the other side of it?"

"The log cabin where Lincoln was born."

"And here?"

"St. Patrick's church, New York."

"And on the reverse?"

"A Russian Orthodox church in Rostov!"

"What's *this?*"

"The door of a castle on the Rhine!"

"And *inside?*"

"A Kansas City soda fountain!"

"And here? And here? And over *there?* And what's *that?*" asks Douglas. "What's this! What about that one! And over *there!*"

It seems as if they are running and rushing and yelling all through the cities, here, there, everywhere, up, down, in, out, climbing, descending, poking, stirring, opening-shutting doors.

"And this, and this, and this, and *this!*"

The night watchman tells all there is to tell.

Their shadows run ahead in narrow alleys, and avenues as broad as rivers made of stone and sand.

They make a great talking circle; they hurry all around and back to where they started.

They are quiet again. The old man is quiet from having said what there was to say, and the producer is quiet from listening and remembering and fitting it all together in his mind. He stands, absent-mindedly fumbling for his cigarette case. It takes him a full minute to open it, examining every action, thinking about it, and to offer the case to the watchman.

"Thanks."

They light up thoughtfully. They puff on their cigarettes and watch the smoke blow away.

Douglas says, "Where's that damned hammer of yours?"

"Here," says Smith.

"You got your nails with you?"

"Yes, sir."

Douglas takes a deep drag on his cigarette and exhales. "Okay, Smith, get to work."

"What?"

"You heard me. Nail what you can back up, on your own time. Most of the stuff that's already torn down is a complete loss. But any bits and pieces that fit and will look decent, put 'em together. Thank God there's a lot still standing. It took me a long time to get it through my head. A man with a nose for business and some imagination, you said. That *is* the world, you said. I should have seen it years ago. Here it all is inside the fence, and me too blind to see what could be done with it. The World Federation in my own back yard and me kicking it over. So help me God, we need more crazy people and night watchmen."

"You know," says the night watchman, "I'm getting old and I'm getting strange. You wouldn't be fooling an old and strange man, would you?"

"I'll make no promises I can't keep," says the producer. "I'll only promise to try. There's a good chance we can go ahead. It would make a beautiful film, there's no doubt of that. We could make it all here, inside the fence, photograph it ten ways from Christmas. There's no doubt about a story, either. You provided it. It's yours. It wouldn't be hard to put some writers to work on it. Good writers. Perhaps only a short subject, twenty minutes, but we could show all the cities and countries here, leaning on and holding each other up. I *like* the idea. I like it very much, believe me. We could show a film like that to anyone anywhere in the world and they'd like it. They couldn't pass it up, it would be too important."

"It's good to hear you talk this way."

"I hope I keep on talking this way," says the producer. "I can't be trusted. I don't trust myself. Hell, I get excited, up one day, down the next. Maybe you'll have to hit me on the head with that hammer to keep me going."

"I'd be pleased," says Smith.

"And *if* we do the film," says the younger man, "I suppose you could help. You know the sets, probably better than anyone. Any suggestions you might want to make, we'd be glad to have. Then, after we do the film, I suppose you won't mind letting us tear the rest of the world down, right?"

"I'd give my permission," says the watchman.

"Well, I'll call off the hounds for a few days and see what happens. Send out a camera crew tomorrow to see what we can line up for shots. Send out some writers. Maybe you can *all* gab. Hell, hell. We'll work it out." Douglas turns toward the gate. "In the meantime, use your hammer all you want. I'll be seeing you. My God, I'm *freezing!*"

They hurry toward the gate. On the way, the old man finds his lunch box where he abandoned it some hours ago. He picks it up, takes out the thermos, and shakes it. "How about a drink before you go?"

"What've you got? Some of that amontillado you were yelling about?"

"1876."

"Let's have some of that, sure."

The thermos is opened and the liquid poured steaming from it into the cup.

"There you are," says the old man.

"Thanks. Here's to you." The producer drinks. "That's good. Ah, that's damned good!"

"It might taste like coffee, but I tell you it's the finest amontillado ever put under a cork."

"You can say *that* again."

The two of them stand among the cities of the world in the moonlight, drinking the hot drink, and the old man remembers something: "There's an old song fits here, a drinking song, I think, a song that all of us who live inside the fence sing, when we're of a mind, when I listen right, and the wind's just right in the telephone wires. It goes like this:

> *"We all go the same way home,*
> *All the same collection, in the same direction,*
> *All go the same way home.*
> *So there's no need to part at all,*
> *And we'll all cling together like the ivy on the*
> *old garden wall . . ."*

They finish drinking the coffee in the middle of Port-au-Prince.

"Hey!" says the producer suddenly. "Take it easy with that cigarette! You want to burn down the whole darn *world?*"

They both look at the cigarette and smile.

"I'll be careful," says Smith.

"So long," says the producer. "I'm *really* late for that party."

"So long, Mr. Douglas."

The gate hasp clicks open and shut, the footsteps die away, the limousine starts up and drives off in the moonlight, leaving behind the cities of the world and an old man standing in the middle of these cities of the world raising his hand to wave.

"So long," says the night watchman.

And then there is only the wind.

19

THE GARBAGE COLLECTOR

THIS IS HOW his work was: he got up at five in the cold dark morning and washed his face with warm water if the heater was working and cold water if the heater was not working. He shaved carefully, talking out to his wife in the kitchen, who was fixing ham and eggs or pancakes or whatever it was that morning. By six o'clock he was driving on his way to work alone, and parking his car in the big yard where all the other men parked their cars as the sun was coming up. The colors of the sky that time of morning were orange and blue and violet and sometimes very red and sometimes yellow or a clear color like water on white rock. Some mornings he could see his breath on the air and some mornings he could not. But as the sun was still rising he knocked his fist on the side of the green truck, and his driver, smiling and saying hello, would climb in the other side of the truck and they would drive out into the great city and go down all the streets until they came to the place where they started work. Sometimes, on the way, they stopped for black coffee and then went on, the warmness in them. And they began the work which meant that he jumped off in front of each house and picked up the garbage cans and brought them back and took off their lids and knocked them against the bin edge, which made the orange peels and cantaloupe rinds and coffee grounds fall out and thump down and begin to fill the empty truck. There were always steak bones and the heads of fish and pieces of green onion and stale celery. If the garbage was new it wasn't so bad, but if it was very old it was bad. He was not sure if he liked the job or not, but it was a job and he did it well, talking about it a lot at some times and sometimes not thinking of it in any way at all. Some days the job was wonderful, for you were out early and the air was cool and fresh until you had worked too long and the sun got hot and the garbage steamed early. But mostly it was a job significant enough to keep him busy and calm and looking at the houses and cut lawns he passed by and seeing how everybody lived. And once or twice a month he was surprised to find that he loved the job and that it was the finest job in the world.

It went on just that way for many years. And then suddenly the job changed for him. It changed in a single day. Later he often wondered how a job could change so much in such a few short hours.

He walked into the apartment and did not see his wife or hear her voice, but she was there, and he walked to a chair and let her stand away from him, watching him as he touched the chair and sat down in it without saying a word. He sat there for a long time.

"What's wrong?" At last her voice came through to him. She must have said it three or four times.

"Wrong?" He looked at this woman and yes, it was his wife all right, it was someone he knew, and this was their apartment with the tall ceilings and the worn carpeting.

"Something happened at work today," he said.

She waited for him.

"On my garbage truck, something happened." His tongue moved dryly on his lips and his eyes shut over his seeing until there was all blackness and no light of any sort and it was like standing alone in a room when you got out of bed in the middle of a dark night. "I think I'm going to quit my job. Try to understand."

"Understand!" she cried.

"It can't be helped. This is all the strangest damned thing that ever happened to me in my life." He opened his eyes and sat there, his hands feeling cold when he rubbed his thumb and forefingers together. "The thing that happened was strange."

"Well, don't just *sit* there!"

146

He took part of a newspaper from the pocket of his leather jacket. "This is today's paper," he said. "December 10, 1951. Los Angeles *Times*. Civil Defense Bulletin. It says they're buying radios for our garbage trucks."

"Well, what's so bad about a little music?"

"No music. You don't understand. No music."

He opened his rough hand and drew with one clean fingernail, slowly, trying to put everything there where he could see it and she could see it. "In this article the mayor says they'll put sending and receiving apparatus on every garbage truck in town." He squinted at his hand. "After the atom bombs hit our city, those radios will talk to us. And then our garbage trucks will go pick up the bodies."

"Well, that seems practical. When———"

"The garbage trucks," he said, "go out and pick up all the bodies."

"You can't just leave bodies around, can you? You've got to take them and———" His wife shut her mouth very slowly. She blinked, one time only, and she did this very slowly also. He watched that one slow blink of her eyes. Then, with a turn of her body, as if someone else had turned it for her, she walked to a chair, paused, thought how to do it, and sat down, very straight and stiff. She said nothing.

He listened to his wrist watch ticking, but with only a small part of his attention.

At last she laughed. "They were joking!"

He shook his head. He felt his head moving from left to right and from right to left, as slowly as everything else had happened. "No. They put a receiver on my truck today. They said, at the alert, if you're working, dump your garbage anywhere. When we radio you, get *in* there and haul out the dead."

Some water in the kitchen boiled over loudly. She let it boil for five seconds and then held the arm of the chair with one hand and got up and found the door and went out. The boiling sound stopped. She stood in the door and then walked back to where he still sat, not moving, his head in one position only.

"It's all blueprinted out. They have squads, sergeants, captains, corporals, everything," he said. "We even know where to *bring* the bodies."

"So you've been thinking about it all day," she said.

"All day since this morning. I thought: Maybe now I don't want to be a garbage collector any more. It used to be Tom and me had fun with a kind of game. You got to do that. Garbage is bad. But if you work at it you can make a game. Tom and me did that. We watched people's garbage. We saw what kind they had. Steak bones in rich houses,

147

lettuce and orange peel in poor ones. Sure it's silly, but a guy's got to make his work as good as he can and worth while or why in hell do it? And you're your own boss, in a way, on a truck . You get out early in the morning and it's an outdoor job, anyway; you see the sun come up and you see the town get up, and that's not bad at all. But now, today, all of a sudden it's not the kind of job for me any more."

His wife started to talk swiftly. She named a lot of things and she talked about a lot more, but before she got very far he cut gently across her talking. "I know, I know, the kids and school, our car, I know," he said. "And bills and money and credit. But what about that farm Dad left us? Why can't we move there, away from cities? I know a little about farming. We could stock up, hole in, have enough to live on for months if anything happened."

She said nothing.

"Sure, all of our friends are here in town," he went on reasonably. "And movies and shows and the kids' friends, and . . ."

She took a deep breath. "Can't we think it over a few more days?"

"I don't know. I'm afraid of that. I'm afraid if I think it over, about my truck and my new work, I'll get used to it. And, oh Christ, it just doesn't seem right a man, a human being, should ever let himself get used to any idea like that."

She shook her head slowly, looking at the windows, the gray walls, the dark pictures on the walls. She tightened her hands. She started to open her mouth.

"I'll think tonight," he said. "I'll stay up awhile. By morning I'll know what to do."

"Be careful with the children. It wouldn't be good, their knowing all this."

"I'll be careful."

"Let's not talk any more, then. I'll finish dinner!" She jumped up and put her hands to her face and then looked at her hands and at the sunlight in the windows. "Why, the kids'll be home any minute."

"I'm not very hungry."

"You got to eat, you just got to keep on going." She hurried off, leaving him alone in the middle of a room where not a breeze stirred the curtains, and only the gray ceiling hung over him with a lonely bulb unlit in it, like an old moon in a sky. He was quiet. He massaged his face with both hands. He got up and stood alone in the dining-room door and walked forward and felt himself sit down and remain seated in a dining-room chair. He saw his hands spread on the white tablecloth, open and empty.

"All afternoon," he said, "I've thought."

She moved through the kitchen, rattling silverware, crashing pans against the silence that was everywhere.

"Wondering," he said, "if you put the bodies in the trucks lengthwise or endwise, with the heads on the right, or the *feet* on the right. Men and women together, or separated? Children in one truck, or mixed with men and women? Dogs in special trucks, or just let them lay? Wondering how *many* bodies one garbage truck can hold. And wondering if you stack them on top of each other and finally knowing you must just have to. I can't figure it. I can't work it out. I try, but there's no guessing, no guessing at all how many you could stack in one single truck."

He sat thinking of how it was late in the day at his work, with the truck full and the canvas pulled over the great bulk of garbage so the bulk shaped the canvas in an uneven mound. And how it was if you suddenly pulled the canvas back and look in. And for a few seconds you saw the white things like macaroni or noodles, only the white things were alive and boiling up, millions of them. And when the white things felt the hot sun on them they simmered down and burrowed and were gone in the lettuce and the old ground beef and the coffee grounds and the heads of white fish. After ten seconds of sunlight the white things that looked like noodles or macaroni were gone and the great bulk of garbage silent and not moving, and you drew the canvas over the bulk and looked at how the canvas folded unevenly over the hidden collection, and underneath you knew it was dark again, and things beginning to move as they must always move when things get dark again.

He was still sitting there in the empty room when the front door of the apartment burst wide. His son and daughter rushed in, laughing, and saw him sitting there, and stopped.

Their mother ran to the kitchen door, held to the edge of it quickly, and stared at her family. They saw her face and they heard her voice:

"Sit down, children, sit down!" She lifted one hand and pushed it toward them. "You're just in time."

20

THE GREAT FIRE

THE MORNING the great fire started, nobody in the house could put it out. It was Mother's niece, Marianne, living with us while her parents were in Europe, who was all aflame. So nobody could smash the little window in the red box at the corner and pull the trigger to bring the gushing hoses and the hatted firemen. Blazing like so much ignited cellophane, Marianne came downstairs, plumped herself with a loud cry or moan at the breakfast table, and refused to eat enough to fill a tooth cavity.

Mother and Father moved away, the warmth in the room being excessive.

"Good morning, Marianne."

"What?" Marianne looked beyond people and spoke vaguely. "Oh, good morning."

"Did you sleep well last night, Marianne?"

But they knew she hadn't slept. Mother gave Marianne a glass of water to drink, and everyone wondered if it would evaporate in her hand. Grandma, from her table chair, surveyed Marianne's fevered eyes. "You're sick, but it's no microbe," she said. "They couldn't find it under a microscope."

"What?" said Marianne.

"Love is godmother to stupidity," said Father detachedly.

"She'll be all right," Mother said to Father. "Girls only seem stupid because when they're in love they can't hear."

"It affects the semicircular canals," said Father. "Making many girls fall right into a fellow's arms. I *know*. I was almost crushed to death once by a falling woman, and let me tell you——"

"Hush." Mother frowned, looking at Marianne. "She can't hear what we're saying; she's cataleptic right now."

"He's coming to pick her up this morning," whispered Mother to Father, as if Marianne wasn't even in the room. "They're going riding in his jalopy."

Father patted his mouth with a napkin. "Was our daughter like this, Mama?" he wanted to know. "She's been married and gone so long, I've forgotten. I don't recall she was so foolish. One would never know a girl had an ounce of sense at a time like this. That's what fools a man. He says, Oh, what a lovely brainless girl, she loves me, I think I'll marry her. He marries her and wakes up one morning and all the dreaminess is gone out of her and her intellect has returned, unpacked, and is hanging up undies all about the house. The man begins running into ropes and lines. He finds himself on a little desert isle, a little living room alone in the midst of a universe, with a honeycomb that has turned into a bear trap, with a butterfly metamorphosed into a wasp. He then immediately takes up a hobby: stamp collecting, lodge meetings, or——"

"How you *do* run on," cried Mother. "Marianne, tell us about this young man. What was his name again? Was it Isak Van Pelt?"

"What? Oh—Isak, yes." Marianne had been roving about her bed all night, sometimes flipping poetry books and reading incredible lines, sometimes lying flat on her back, sometimes on her tummy looking out at dreaming moonlit country. The smell of jasmine had touched the room all night and the excessive warmth of early spring (the thermometer read fifty-five degrees) had kept her awake. She looked like a dying moth, if anyone had peeked through the keyhole.

This morning she had clapped her hands over her head in the mirror and come to breakfast, remembering just in time to put on a dress.

Grandma laughed quietly all during breakfast. Finally she

151

said, "You must eat, child, you *must.*" So Marianne played with her toast and got half a piece down. Just then there was a loud honk outside. That was Isak! In his jalopy!

"Whoop!" cried Marianne, and ran upstairs quickly.

The young Isak Van Pelt was brought in and introduced around.

When Marianne was finally gone, Father sat down, wiping his forehead. "I don't know. This is too much."

"You were the one who suggested she start going out," said Mother.

"And I'm sorry I suggested it," he said. "But she's been visiting us for six months now, and six more months to go. I thought if she met some nice young man——"

"And they were married," husked Grandma darkly, "why, Marianne might move out almost immediately—is *that* it?"

"Well," said Father.

"Well," said Grandma.

"But now it's worse than before," said Father. "She floats around singing with her eyes shut, playing those infernal love records and talking to herself. A man can stand so much. She's getting so she laughs all the time, too. Do eighteen-year-old girls often wind up in the booby hatch?"

"He seems a nice young man," said Mother.

"Yes, we can always pray for that," said Father, taking out a little shot glass. "Here's to an early marriage."

The second morning Marianne was out of the house like a fireball when first she heard the jalopy horn. There was no time for the young man even to come to the door. Only Grandma saw them roar off together, from the parlor window.

"She almost knocked me down." Father brushed his mustache. "What's *that?* Brained eggs? Well."

In the afternoon, Marianne, home again, drifted about the living room to the phonograph records. The needle hiss filled the house. She played "That Old Black Magic" twenty-one times, going "la la la" as she swam with her eyes closed in the room.

"I'm afraid to go in my own parlor," said Father. "I retired from business to smoke cigars and enjoy living, not to have a limp relative humming about under the parlor chandelier."

"Hush," said Mother.

"This is a crisis," announced Father, "in my life. After all, she's just visiting."

"You know how visiting girls are. Away from home they think they're in Paris, France. She'll be gone in October. It's not so dreadful."

"Let's see," figured Father slowly. "I'll have been buried

152

just about one hundred and thirty days out at Green Lawn Cemetery by then." He got up and threw his paper down into a little white tent on the floor. "By George, Mother, I'm talking to her right *now!*"

He went and stood in the parlor door, peering through it at the waltzing Marianne. "La," she sang to the music.

Clearing his throat, he stepped through.

"Marianne," he said.

" 'That old black magic . . .' " sang Marianne. "Yes?"

He watched her hands swinging in the air. She gave him a sudden fiery look as she danced by.

"I want to talk to you." He straightened his tie.

"Dah dum dee dum dum dee dum dee dum dum," she sang.

"Did you *hear* me?" he demanded.

"He's *so* nice," she said.

"Evidently."

"Do you know, he bows and opens doors like a doorman and plays a trumpet like Harry James and brought me daisies this morning?"

"I wouldn't doubt."

"His eyes are blue." She looked at the ceiling.

He could find nothing at all on the ceiling to look at.

She kept looking, as she danced, at the ceiling as he came over and stood near her, looking up, but there wasn't a rain spot or a settling crack there, and he sighed, "Marianne."

"And we ate lobster at that river café."

"Lobster. I know, but we don't want you breaking down, getting weak. One day, tomorrow, you must stay home and help your aunt Math make her doilies——"

"Yes, sir." She dreamed around the room with her wings out.

"Did you *hear* me?" he demanded.

"Yes," she whispered. "Yes." Her eyes shut. "Oh yes, yes." Her skirts whished around. "Uncle," she said, her head back, lolling.

"You'll help your aunt with her doilies?" he cried.

"—with her doilies," she murmured.

"There!" He sat down in the kitchen, plucking up the paper. "I guess *I* told her!"

But next morning he was on the edge of his bed when he heard the hot-rod's thunderous muffler and heard Marianne fall downstairs, linger two seconds in the dining room for breakfast, hesitate by the bathroom long enough to consider whether she would be sick, and then the slam of the front door, the sound of the jalopy banging down the street, two people singing off key in it.

Father put his head in his hands. "Doilies," he said.

"What?" said Mother.

"Dooley's," said Father. "I'm going down to Dooley's for a morning visit."

"But Dooley's isn't open until ten."

"I'll wait," decided Father, eyes shut.

That night and seven other wild nights the porch swing sang a little creaking song, back and forth, back and forth. Father, hiding in the living room, could be seen in fierce relief whenever he drafted his ten-cent cigar and the cherry light illumined his immensely tragic face. The porch swing creaked. He waited for another creak. He heard little butterfly-soft sounds from outside, little palpitations of laughter and sweet nothings in small ears. "My porch," said Father. "My swing," he whispered to his cigar, looking at it. "My house." He listened for another creak. "My God," he said.

He went to the tool shed and appeared on the dark porch with a shiny oil can. "No, don't get up. Don't bother. There, and there." He oiled the swing joints. It was dark. He couldn't see Marianne; he could smell her. The perfume almost knocked him off into the rosebush. He couldn't see her gentleman friend, either. "Good night," he said. He went in and sat down and there was no more creaking. Now all he could hear was something that sounded like the mothlike flutter of Marianne's heart.

"He must be very nice," said Mother in the kitchen door, wiping a dinner dish.

"That's what I'm hoping," whispered Father. "That's why I let them have the porch every night!"

"So many days in a row," said Mother. "A girl doesn't go with a nice young man that many times unless he's serious."

"Maybe he'll propose tonight!" was Father's happy thought.

"Hardly so soon. And she is so young."

"Still," he ruminated, "it might happen. It's *got* to happen, by the Lord Harry."

Grandma chuckled from her corner easy chair. It sounded like someone turning the pages of an ancient book.

"What's so funny?" said Father.

"Wait and see," said Grandma. "Tomorrow."

Father stared at the dark, but Grandma would say no more.

"Well, well," said Father at breakfast. He surveyed his eggs with a kindly, paternal eye. "Well, well, by gosh, last night, on the porch, there was *more whispering*. What's his name? Isak? Well, now, if I'm any judge at all, I think he proposed to Marianne last night; yes, I'm positive of it!"

"It would be nice," said Mother. "A spring marriage. But it's so *soon*."

"Look," said Father with full-mouthed logic. "Marianne's the kind of girl who marries quick and young. We can't stand in her way, can we?"

"For once I think you're right," said Mother. "A marriage would be fine. Spring flowers, and Marianne looking nice in that gown I saw at Haydecker's last week."

They all peered anxiously at the stairs, waiting for Marianne to appear.

"Pardon me," rasped Grandma, sighting up from her morning toast. "But I wouldn't talk of getting rid of Marianne just yet if I were you."

"And why not?"

"Because."

"Because why?"

"I hate to spoil your plans," rustled Grandma, chuckling. She gestured with her little vinegary head. "But while you people were worrying about getting Marianne married, I've been keeping tab on her. Seven days now I've been watching this young fellow each day he came in his car and honked his horn outside. He must be an actor or a quick-change artist or something."

"What?" asked Father.

"Yep," said Grandma. "Because one day he was a young blond fellow, and next day he was a tall dark fellow, and Wednesday he was a chap with a brown mustache, and Thursday he had wavy red hair, and Friday he was shorter, with a Chevrolet stripped down instead of a Ford."

Mother and Father sat for a minute as if hit with hammers right behind the left ear.

At last Father, his face exploding with color, shouted, "Do you mean to *say!* You *sat* there, woman, you say; all those men, and you——"

"You were always hiding," snapped Grandma. "So you wouldn't spoil things. If you'd come out in the open you'd have seen the same as I. I never said a word. She'll simmer down. It's just her time of life. Every woman goes through it. It's hard, but they can survive. A new man every day does wonders for a girl's ego!"

"You, you, you, you, *you!*" Father choked on it, eyes wild, throat gorged too big for his collar. He fell back in his chair, exhausted. Mother sat, stunned.

"Good morning, everyone!" Marianne raced downstairs and popped into a chair. Father stared at her.

"You, you, you, you, you," he accused Grandma.

I shall run down the street shouting, thought Father wildly, and break the fire-alarm window and pull the lever and bring the fire engines and the hoses. Or perhaps there will be a

155

late snowstorm and I shall set Marianne out in it to cool.

He did neither. The heat in the room being excessive, according to the wall calendar, everyone moved out onto the cool porch while Marianne sat looking at her orange juice.

21

HAIL AND FAREWELL

BUT OF COURSE he was going away, there was nothing else to do, the time was up, the clock had run out, and he was going very far away indeed. His suitcase was packed, his shoes were shined, his hair was brushed, he had expressly washed behind his ears, and it remained only for him to go down the stairs, out the front door, and up the street to the small-town station where the train would make a stop for him alone. Then Fox Hill, Illinois, would be left far off in his past. And he would go on, perhaps to Iowa, perhaps to Kansas, perhaps even to California; a small boy, twelve years old with a birth certificate in his valise to show he had been born forty-three years ago.

"Willie!" called a voice downstairs.

"Yes!" He hoisted his suitcase. In his bureau mirror he saw a face made of June dandelions and July apples and warm summer-morning milk. There, as always, was his look of the angel and the innocent, which might never, in the years of his life, change.

"Almost time," called the woman's voice.

"All right!" And he went down the stairs, grunting and smiling. In the living room sat Anna and Steve, their clothes painfully neat.

"Here I am!" cried Willie in the parlor door.

Anna looked like she was going to cry. "Oh, good Lord, you can't really be leaving us, can you, Willie?"

"People are beginning to talk," said Willie quietly. "I've been here three years now. But when people begin to talk, I know it's time to put on my shoes and buy a railway ticket."

"It's all so strange. I don't understand. It's so sudden," Anna said. "Willie, we'll miss you."

"I'll write you every Christmas, so help me. Don't you write me."

"It's been a great pleasure and satisfaction," said Steve, sitting there, his words the wrong size in his mouth. "It's a shame it had to stop. It's a shame you had to tell us about yourself. It's an awful shame you can't stay on."

"You're the nicest folks I ever had," said Willie, four feet high, in no need of a shave, the sunlight on his face.

And then Anna *did* cry. "Willie, Willie." And she sat down and looked as if she wanted to hold him but was afraid to hold him now; she looked at him with shock and amazement and her hands empty, not knowing what to do with him now.

"It's not easy to go," said Willie. "You get used to things. You want to stay. But it doesn't work. I tried to stay on once after people began to suspect. 'How horrible!' people said. 'All these years, playing with our innocent children,' they said, 'and us not guessing! Awful!' they said. And finally I had to just leave town one night. It's not easy. You know darned well how much I love both of you. Thanks for three swell years."

They all went to the front door. "Willie, where're you going?"

"I don't know. I just start traveling. When I see a town that looks green and nice, I settle in."

"Will you ever come back?"

"Yes," he said earnestly with his high voice. "In about twenty years it should begin to show in my face. When it does, I'm going to make a grand tour of all the mothers and fathers I've ever had."

They stood on the cool summer porch, reluctant to say the last words. Steve was looking steadily at an elm tree. "How many other folks've you stayed with, Willie? How many adoptions?"

Willie figured it, pleasantly enough. "I guess it's about five towns and five couples and over twenty years gone by since I started my tour."

"Well, we can't holler," said Steve. "Better to've had a son thirty-six months than none whatever."

"Well," said Willie, and kissed Anna quickly, seized at his luggage, and was gone up the street in the green noon light, under the trees, a very young boy indeed, not looking back, running steadily.

The boys were playing on the green park diamond when he came by. He stood a little while among the oak-tree shadows, watching them hurl the white, snowy baseball into the warm summer air, saw the baseball shadow fly like a dark bird over the grass, saw their hands open in mouths to catch this swift piece of summer that now seemed most especially important to hold onto. The boys' voices yelled. The ball lit on the grass near Willie.

Carrying the ball forward from under the shade trees, he thought of the last three years now spent to the penny, and the five years before that, and so on down the line to the year when he was really eleven and twelve and fourteen and the voices saying: "What's wrong with Willie, missus?" "Mrs. B., is Willie late a-growin'?" "Willie, you smokin' cigars lately?" The echoes died in summer light and color. His mother's voice: "Willie's twenty-one today!" And a thousand voices saying: "Come back, son, when you're fifteen; *then* maybe we'll give you a job."

He stared at the baseball in his trembling hand, as if it were his life, an interminable ball of years strung around and around and around, but always leading back to his twelfth birthday. He heard the kids walking toward him; he felt them blot out the sun, and they were older, standing around him.

"Willie! Where you goin'?" They kicked his suitcase.

How tall they stood in the sun. In the last few months it seemed the sun had passed a hand above their heads, beckoned, and they were warm metal drawn melting upward; they were golden taffy pulled by an immense gravity to the sky, thirteen, fourteen years old, looking down upon Willie, smiling, but already beginning to neglect him. It had started four months ago:

"Choose up sides! Who wants Willie?"

"Aw, Willie's too little; we don't play with 'kids.' "

And they raced ahead of him, drawn by the moon and the sun and the turning seasons of leaf and wind, and he was twelve years old and not of them any more. And the other voices beginning again on the old, the dreadfully familiar, the cool refrain: "Better feed that boy vitamins, Steve." "Anna, does shortness *run* in your family?" And the cold fist knocking at your heart again and knowing that the roots would

159

have to be pulled up again after so many good years with the "folks."

"Willie, where you goin'?"

He jerked his head. He was back among the towering, shadowing boys who milled around him like giants at a drinking fountain bending down.

"Goin' a few days visitin' a cousin of mine."

"Oh." There was a day, a year ago, when they would have cared very much indeed. But now there was only curiosity for his luggage, their enchantment with trains and trips and far places.

"How about a coupla fast ones?" said Willie.

They looked doubtful, but, considering the circumstances, nodded. He dropped his bag and ran out; the white baseball was up in the sun, away to their burning white figures in the far meadow, up in the sun again, rushing, life coming and going in a pattern. Here, *there!* Mr. and Mrs. Robert Hanlon, Creek Bend, Wisconsin, 1932, the first couple, the first year! Here, there! Henry and Alice Boltz, Limeville, Iowa, 1935! The baseball flying. The Smiths, the Eatons, the Robinsons! 1939! 1945! Husband and wife, husband and wife, husband and wife, no children, no children! A knock on this door, a knock on that.

"Pardon me. My name is William. I wonder if——"

"A sandwich? Come in, sit down. Where you *from*, son?"

The sandwich, a tall glass of cold milk, the smiling, the nodding, the comfortable, leisurely talking.

"Son, you look like you been traveling. You run *off* from somewhere?"

"No."

"Boy, are you an orphan?"

Another glass of milk.

"We always wanted kids. It never worked out. Never knew why. One of those things. Well, well. It's getting late, son. Don't you think you better hit for home?"

"Got no home."

"A boy like you? Not dry behind the ears? Your mother'll be worried."

"Got no home and no folks anywhere in the world. I wonder if—I wonder—could I sleep here tonight?"

"Well, now, son, I don't just know. We never considered taking in——" said the husband.

"We got chicken for supper tonight," said the wife, "enough for extras, enough for company. . . ."

And the years turning and flying away, the voices, and the faces, and the people, and always the same first conversations. The voice of Emily Robinson, in her rocking chair, in summer-night darkness, the last night he stayed with her, the night she discovered his secret, her voice saying:

"I look at all the little children's faces going by. And I sometimes think, What a shame, what a shame, that all these flowers have to be cut, all these bright fires have to be put out. What a shame these, all of these you see in schools or running by, have to get tall and unsightly and wrinkle and turn gray or get bald, and finally, all bone and wheeze, be dead and buried off away. When I hear them laugh I can't believe they'll ever go the road I'm going. Yet here they *come!* I still remember Wordsworth's poem: 'When all at once I saw a crowd, A host of golden daffodils; Beside the lake, beneath the trees, Fluttering and dancing in the breeze.' That's how I think of children, cruel as they sometimes are, mean as I know they can be, but not yet showing the meanness around their eyes or *in* their eyes, not yet full of tiredness. They're so eager for everything! I guess that's what I miss most in older folks, the eagerness gone nine times out of ten, the freshness gone, so much of the drive and life down the drain. I like to watch school let out each day. It's like someone threw a bunch of flowers out the school front doors. How does it feel, Willie? How does it feel to be young forever? To look like a silver dime new from the mint? Are you happy? Are you as fine as you *seem?*"

The baseball whizzed from the blue sky, stung his hand like a great pale insect. Nursing it, he hears his memory say:

"I worked with what I had. After my folks died, after I found I couldn't get man's work anywhere, I tried carnivals, but they only laughed. 'Son,' they said, you're not a midget, and even if you are, you look like a *boy!* We want midgets with midgets' *faces!* Sorry, son, sorry.' So I left home, started out, thinking: What *was* I? A boy. I looked like a boy, sounded like a boy, so I might as well go on being a boy. No use fighting it. No use screaming. So what could I do? What job was handy? And then one day I saw this man in a restaurant looking at another man's pictures of his children. 'Sure wish I had kids,' he said. 'Sure wish I had kids.' He kept shaking his head. And me sitting a few seats away from him, a hamburger in my hands. I sat there, *frozen!* At that very instant I knew what my job would be for all the rest of my life. There *was* work for me, after all. Making lonely people happy. Keeping myself busy. Playing forever. I knew I had to play forever. Deliver a few papers, run a few errands, mow a few lawns, maybe. But *hard* work? No. All I had to do was be a mother's son and a father's pride. I turned to the man down the counter from me. 'I beg your pardon,' I said. I *smiled* at him. . . ."

"But, Willie," said Mrs. Emily long ago, "didn't you ever get lonely? Didn't you ever want—*things*—that grownups wanted?"

"I fought that out alone," said Willie. "I'm a boy, I told myself, I'll have to live in a boy's world, read boys' books, play boys' games, cut myself off from everything else. I can't be both. I got to be only one thing—young. And so I played that way. Oh, it wasn't easy. There were times——" He lapsed into silence.

"And the family you lived with, they never knew?"

"No. Telling them would have spoiled everything. I told them I was a runaway; I let them check through official channels, police. Then, when there was no record, let them put in to adopt me. That was best of all; as long as they never guessed. But then, after three years, or five years, they guessed, or a traveling man came through, or a carnival man saw me, and it was over. It always had to end."

"And you're very happy and it's nice being a child for over forty years?"

"It's a living, as they say. And when you make other people happy, then you're almost happy too. I got my job to do and I do it. And anyway, in a few years now I'll be in my second childhood. All the fevers will be out of me and all the unfulfilled things and most of the dreams. Then I can relax, maybe, and play the role all the way."

He threw the baseball one last time and broke the reverie. Then he was running to seize his luggage. Tom, Bill, Jamie, Bob, Sam—their names moved on his lips. They were embarrassed at his shaking hands.

"After all, Willie, it ain't as if you're going to China or Timbuktu."

"That's right, isn't it?" Willie did not move.

"So long, Willie. See you next week!"

"So long, so long!"

And he was walking off with his suitcase again, looking at the trees, going away from the boys and the street where he had lived, and as he turned the corner a train whistle screamed, and he began to run.

The last thing he saw and heard was a white ball tossed at a high roof, back and forth, back and forth, and two voices crying out as the ball pitched now up, down, and back through the sky, "Annie, annie, over! Annie, annie, over!" like the crying of birds flying off to the far south.

In the early morning, with the smell of the mist and the cold metal, with the iron smell of the train around him and a full night of traveling shaking his bones and his body, and a smell of the sun beyond the horizon, he awoke and looked

162

out upon a small town just arising from sleep. Lights were coming on, soft voices muttered, a red signal bobbed back and forth, back and forth in the cold air. There was that sleeping hush in which echoes are dignified by clarity, in which echoes stand nakedly alone and sharp. A porter moved by, a shadow in shadows.

"Sir," said Willie.

The porter stopped.

"What town's this?" whispered the boy in the dark.

"Valleyville."

"How many people?"

"Ten thousand. Why? This your stop?"

"It looks green." Willie gazed out at the cold morning town for a long time. "It looks nice and quiet," said Willie.

"Son," said the porter, "you know where you *going?*"

"Here," said Willie, and got up quietly in the still, cool, iron-smelling morning, in the train dark, with a rustling and stir.

"I hope you know what you're doing, boy," said the porter.

"Yes, sir," said Willie. "I know what I'm doing." And he was down the dark aisle, luggage lifted after him by the porter, and out in the smoking, steaming-cold, beginning-to-lighten morning. He stood looking up at the porter and the black metal train against the few remaining stars. The train gave a great wailing blast of whistle, the porters cried out all along the line, the cars jolted, and his special porter waved and smiled down at the boy there, the small boy there with the big luggage who shouted up to him, even as the whistle screamed again.

"What?" shouted the porter, hand cupped to ear.

"Wish me luck!" cried Willie.

"Best of luck, son," called the porter, waving, smiling. "Best of luck, boy!"

"Thanks," said Willie, in the great sound of the train, in the steam and roar.

He watched the black train until it was completely gone away and out of sight. He did not move all the time it was going. He stood quietly, a small boy twelve years old, on the worn wooden platform, and only after three entire minutes did he turn at last to face the empty streets below.

Then, as the sun was rising, he began to walk very fast, so as to keep warm, down into the new town.

22

THE GOLDEN APPLES OF THE SUN

"South," said the captain.

"But," said his crew, "there simply *aren't* any directions out here in space."

"When you travel on down toward the sun," replied the captain, "and everything gets yellow and warm and lazy, then you're going in one direction only." He shut his eyes and thought about the smoldering, warm, faraway land, his breath moving gently in his mouth. "South." He nodded slowly to himself. "South."

Their rocket was the *Copa de Oro*, also named the *Prometheus* and the *Icarus*, and their destination in all reality was the blazing noonday sun. In high good spirits they had packed along two thousand sour lemonades and a thousand white-capped beers for this journey to the wide Sahara. And now as the sun boiled up at them they remembered a score of verses and quotations:

" 'The golden apples of the sun'?"

"Yeats."

" 'Fear no more the heat of the sun'?"

"Shakespeare, of course!"

" 'Cup of Gold'? Steinbeck. 'The Crock of Gold'? Stephens. And what about the pot of gold at the rainbow's end? *There's* a name for our trajectory, by God. Rainbow!"

"Temperature?"

"One thousand degrees Fahrenheit!"

The captain stared from the huge dark-lensed port, and there indeed was the sun, and to go to that sun and touch it and steal part of it forever away was his quiet and single idea. In this ship were combined the coolly delicate and the coldly practical. Through corridors of ice and milk-frost, ammoniated winter and storming snowflakes blew. Any spark from that vast hearth burning out there beyond the callous hull of this ship, any small firebreath that might seep through would find winter, slumbering here like all the coldest hours of February.

The audio-thermometer murmured in the arctic silence: "Temperature: two thousand degrees!"

Falling, thought the captain, like a snowflake into the lap of June, warm July, and the sweltering dog-mad days of August.

"Three thousand degrees Fahrenheit!"

Under the snow fields engines raced, refrigerants pumped ten thousand miles per hour in rimed boa-constrictor coils.

"Four thousand degrees Fahrenheit."

Noon. Summer. July.

"Five thousand Fahrenheit!"

And at last the captain spoke with all the quietness of the journey in his voice:

"Now, we are touching the sun."

Their eyes, thinking it, were melted gold.

"Seven thousand degrees!"

Strange how a mechanical thermometer could sound excited, though it possessed only an emotionless steel voice.

"What *time* is it?" asked someone.

Everyone had to smile.

For now there was only the sun and the sun and the sun. It was every horizon, it was every direction. It burned the minutes, the seconds, the hourglasses, the clocks; it burned all time and eternity away. It burned the eyelids and the serum of the dark world behind the lids, the retina, the hidden brain; and it burned sleep and the sweet memories of sleep and cool nightfall.

"Watch it!"

"Captain!"

Bretton, the first mate, fell flat to the winter deck. His protective suit whistled where, burst open, his warmness, his oxygen, and his life bloomed out in a frosted steam.

"Quick!"

Inside Bretton's plastic face-mask, milk crystals had already gathered in blind patterns. They bent to see.

"A structural defect in his suit, Captain. Dead."

"Frozen."

They stared at that other thermometer which showed how winter lived in this snowing ship. One thousand degrees below zero. The captain gazed down upon the frosted statue and the twinkling crystals that iced over it as he watched. Irony of the coolest sort, he thought; a man afraid of fire and killed by frost.

The captain turned away. "No time. No time. Let him lie." He felt his tongue move. "Temperature?"

The dials jumped four thousand degrees.

"Look. Will you look? Look."

Their icicle was melting.

The captain jerked his head to look at the ceiling.

As if a motion-picture projector had jammed a single clear memory frame in his head, he found his mind focused ridiculously on a scene whipped out of childhood.

Spring mornings as a boy he found he had leaned from his bedroom window into the snow-smelling air to see the sun sparkle the last icicle of winter. A dripping of white wine, the blood of cool but warming April fell from that clear crystal blade. Minute by minute, December's weapon grew less dangerous. And then at last the icicle fell with the sound of a single chime to the graveled walk below.

"Auxiliary pump's broken, sir. Refrigeration. We're losing our ice!"

A shower of warm rain shivered down upon them. The captain jerked his head right and left. "Can you see the trouble? Christ, don't stand there, we haven't time!"

The men rushed; the captain bent in the warm rain, cursing, felt his hands run over the cold machine, felt them burrow and search, and while he worked he saw a future which was removed from them by the merest breath. He saw the skin peel from the rocket beehive, men, thus revealed, running, running, mouths shrieking, soundless. Space was a black mossed well where life drowned its roars and terrors. Scream a big scream, but space snuffed it out before it was half up your throat. Men scurried, ants in a flaming matchbox; the ship was dripping lava, gushing steam, nothing!

"Captain?"

The nightmare flicked away.

"Here." He worked in the soft warm rain that fell from the upper decks. He fumbled at the auxiliary pump. "Damn it!" He jerked the feed line. When it came, it'd be the quickest death in the history of dying. One moment, yelling; a warm flash later only the billion billion tons of space-fire

166

would whisper, unheard, in space. Popped like strawberries in a furnace, while their thoughts lingered on the scorched air a long breath after their bodies were charred roast and fluorescent gas.

"Dam!" He stabbed the auxiliary pump with a screw driver. "Jesus!" He shuddered. The complete annihilation of it. He clamped his eyes shut, teeth tight. God, he thought, we're used to more leisurely dyings, measured in minutes and hours. Even twenty seconds now would be a slow death compared to this hungry idiot thing waiting to eat us!

"Captain, do we pull out or stay?"

"Get the Cup ready. Take over, finish this. Now!"

He turned and put his hand to the working mechanism of the huge Cup; shoved his fingers into the robot Glove. A twitch of his hand here moved a gigantic hand, with gigantic metal fingers, from the bowels of the ship. Now, now, the great metal hand slid out holding the huge *Copa de Oro*, breathless, into the iron furnace, the bodiless body and the fleshless flesh of the sun.

A mililon years ago, though the captain, quickly, quickly, as he moved the hand and the Cup, a million years ago a naked man on a lonely northern trail saw lightning strike a tree. And while his clan fled, with bare hands he plucked a limb of fire, broiling the flesh of his fingers, to carry it, running in triumph, shielding it from the rain with his body, to his cave, where he shrieked out a laugh and tossed it full on a mound of leaves and gave his people summer. And the tribe crept at last, trembling, near the fire, and they put out their flinching hands and felt the new season in their cave, this small yellow spot of changing weather, and they, too, at last, nervously, smiled. And the gift of fire was theirs.

"Captain!"

It took all of four seconds for the huge hand to push the empty Cup to the fire. So here we are again, today, on another trail, he thought, reaching for a cup of precious gas and vacuum, a handful of different fire with which to run back up cold space, lighting our way, and take to Earth a gift of fire that might burn forever. Why?

He knew the answer before the question.

Because the atoms we work with our hands, on Earth, are pitiful; the atomic bomb is pitiful and small and our knowledge is pitiful and small, and only the sun really knows what we want to know, and only the sun has the secret. And besides, it's fun, it's a chance, it's a great thing coming here, playing tag, hitting and running. There is no reason, really except the pride and vanity of little insect men hoping to sting the lion and escape the maw. My God, we'll say, we *did* it! And here is our cup of energy, fire, vibration, cal' it what you will, that may well power our cities and sail our ships and light our libraries and tan our children and bake our daily breads and simmer the knowledge of our universe for us for a thousand years until it is well done. Here, from this cup, all good men of science and religion: drink! Warm yourselves against the night of ignorance, the long snows of superstition, the cold winds of disbelief, and from the great fear of darkness in each man. So: we stretch out our hand with the beggar's cup . . ."

"Ah."

The Cup dipped into the sun. It scooped up a bit of the flesh of God, the blood of the universe, the blazing thought, the blinding philosophy that set out and mothered a galaxy, that idled and swept planets in their fields and summoned or laid to rest lives and livelihoods.

"Now, *slow*," whispered the captain.

"What'll happen when we pull it inside? That extra heat now, at this time, Captain?"

"God knows."

"Auxiliary pump all repaired, sir."

"Start it!"

The pump leaped on.

"Close the lid of the Cup and inside now, slow, slow."

The beautiful hand outside the ship trembled, a tremendous image of his own gesture, sank with oiled silence into the ship body. The Cup, lid shut, dripped yellow flowers and white stars, slid deep. The audio-thermometer screamed. The refrigerator system kicked; ammoniated fluids banged the walls like blood in the head of a shrieking idiot.

He shut the outer air-lock door.

"Now."

They waited. The ship's pulse ran. The heart of the ship rushed, beat, rushed, the Cup of gold in it. The cold blood raced around about down through, around about down through.

The captain exhaled slowly.

The ice stopped dripping from the ceiling. It froze again.

"Let's get out of here."

The ship turned and ran.

"Listen!"

The heart of the ship was slowing, slowing. The dials spun on down through the thousands; the needles whirred, invisible. The thermometer voice chanted the change of seasons. They were all thinking now, together: Pull away and away from the fire and the flame, the heat and the melting, the yellow and the white. Go on out now to cool and dark. In twenty hours perhaps they might even dismantle some refrigerators, let winter die. Soon they would move in night so cold it might be necessary to use the ship's new furnace, draw heat from the shielded fire they carried now like an unborn child.

They were going home.

They were going home and there was some little time, even as he tended to the body of Bretton lying in a bank of white winter snow, for the captain to remember a poem he had written many years before:

> *Sometimes I see the sun a burning Tree,*
> *Its golden fruit swung bright in airless air,*
> *Its apples wormed with man and gravity,*
> *Their worship breathing from them everywhere,*
> *As man sees Sun as burning Tree . . .*

The captain sat for a long while by the body, feeling many separate things. I feel sad, he thought, and I feel good, and I feel like a boy coming home from school with a handful of dandelions.

"Well," said the captain, sitting, eyes shut, sighing. "Well, where do we go now, eh, where are we going?" He felt his men sitting or standing all about him, the terror dead in them, their breathing quiet. "When you've gone a long, long way down to the sun and touched it and lingered and jumped around and streaked away from it, where are you going then? When you go away from the heat and the noonday light and the laziness, where do you go?"

His men waited for him to say it out. They waited for him to gather all of the coolness and the whiteness and the welcome and refreshing climate of the word in his mind, and they saw him settle the word, like a bit of ice cream, in his mouth, rolling it gently.

"There's only one direction in space from here on out," he said at last.

They waited. They waited as the ship moved swiftly into cold darkness away from the light.

"North," murmured the captain. "North."

And they all smiled, as if a wind had come up suddenly in the middle of a hot afternoon.

ABOUT THE AUTHOR

RAY BRADBURY was born in Waukegan, Illinois, in 1920. He has published over 300 stories during the past twenty-five years, and fourteen books including stories and novels. He wrote the screenplay for John Huston's *Moby Dick*, and his own novel, *Fahrenheit 451*, has been made into a motion picture by François Truffaut. His more recent books include *S Is for Space*, *The Vintage Bradbury* and *Twice 22*. Mr. Bradbury lives in Los Angeles, California.